THE BEST
ADVICE EVER

FOR

GOLFERS

THE BEST
ADVICE EVER

FOR

GOLFERS

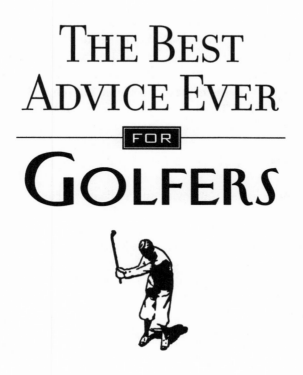

ROBERT McCORD

**Andrews McMeel
Publishing**

Kansas City

01 02 03 04 05 QUF 10 9 8 7 6 5 4 3 2 1

Library of Congress Cataloging-in-Publication Data

McCord, Robert R.
    The best advice ever for golfers / Robert McCord.
        p. cm.
    ISBN 0-7407-1010-9
    1. Golf-Miscellanea. I. Title.
GV967 .M215 2001
796.352—dc21

00-054736

For Susan and John Hanley;
and Bob, April, and Joe Hanley

For Barbara McCord; and Steve, Candace,
Sam, Janet, Mathew, and Kimberly McCord

In loving memory to:
Helen Reed and Richard S. McCord,
my parents; Frank Reed McCord, my brother,
and Nancy Unger McCord, my wife

ACKNOWLEDGMENTS

*Many thanks to Allan Stark, founding editor
of Stark Books, who suggested I write this book
and encouraged me through completion*

*Thanks to Kelly Gilbert and Patrick Dobson
and the rest of the staff at Stark Books
and Andrews McMeel Publishing*

*Also a note of appreciation to my agent,
David McCormick at IMG,
the founding captain of
The Speckled Hens golf team*

CONTENTS

Prologue...ix

Fully analyzed and experienced, golf is an elegantly complex yet simple game. Hit the ball into the hole in as few strokes as possible. What could be more basic? Today we have an abundance of professional instructors and a variety of media imparting the wisdom and advice required to learn and appreciate the game. Every year, millions of words and images are offered to us through books, magazines, videos, the Internet, and other media in a relentless effort to help us take dead aim. This book is a focused attempt to provide you with a gourmet sampler of some of the best golf advice from those who have contributed to the game over the years.

In the beginning, the Scots dominated organized golf. The first golf club, the Honorable Company of Edinburgh Golfers, was founded in 1744. The original rules of golf numbered thirteen and were defined by The Royal and Ancient Golf Club of St. Andrews, which was established in 1754. Tournaments were largely match play events among club members. The first major championship, the British Open, was held at Prestwick, Scotland, in 1860. Willie Park won that event with a 36-hole score of 174. The Open would be held in Scotland for its first thirty-four years.

In the early days golf wisdom was largely passed down by word of mouth. The club professional was likely to be the instructor, greenskeeper, ball maker, club maker, caddie master, and general jack-of-all-trades. He made extra money in challenge matches and might design a golf course or two. Among the early golf heroes are professionals Alan Robertson, Old Tom Morris, Young Tom Morris, Willie Park, Willie Park, Jr., and Harry Vardon. They became ambassadors for golf by playing in tournaments, teaching, authoring instructional books, developing lines of golf merchandise, and traveling abroad to win fortune and promote the game. Old Tom Morris, Willie Park, Jr., and others such as Donald Ross and Alister Mackenzie became noteworthy course architects. Harry Vardon was one of golf's first international promoters when he made a 20,000-mile, nine-month promotional tour of North America in 1900. Sponsored by A. G. Spalding, which manufactured the Vardon Flyer golf ball, he participated in exhibitions and other golf marketing activities. Vardon took time out in 1900 to win the U.S. Open at the Chicago Golf Club in Wheaton, Illinois. At the conclusion of his North American visit he noted: "I like the country, the golfers, and their links. They are not yet up to the class of the leading amateurs in England and Scotland."

Golf has been played in the United States since at least the eighteenth century but it was not until the end of the 1800s that the sport began to flourish in North America. The Royal Montreal Golf Club was founded in 1873. The United States Golf Association was established in 1894 with St. Andrews, The Country Club, The Chicago Golf Club, Shinnecock Hills, and Newport its founding members. The first U.S. Amateur and the inaugural U.S. Open were both played at the Newport, Rhode Island, Golf Club in 1895.

Early on, foreign-born players dominated American professional golf. Willie Anderson, a native-born Scotsman, won four National Opens, three of them in a row (1903–1905) before he died at age thirty. (Only Americans Bobby Jones, Ben Hogan, and Jack Nicklaus have equaled that record.) Johnny McDermott become the first American-born player to win the Open. He won in 1911 and again in 1912. But it was Francis Ouimet, an amateur from Massachusetts, who vastly increased the popularity of golf in

America by defeating veteran professionals Harry Vardon and Ted Ray in an eighteen-hole playoff in the 1913 U.S. Open at The Country Club. In 1921 Jock Hutchison become the first American citizen to win the British Open, signaling that the Americans had arrived on the international golf scene. Nine years later, Bobby Jones, a golf prodigy from Georgia, swept the four major tournaments of his day, the British Open, British Amateur, U.S. Open, and the U.S. Amateur, then he retired at age twenty-eight.

By 1900 there were approximately 1,000 golf courses in the United States. Regional associations such as The Metropolitan Golf Association (1897), The Pacific Northwest Golf Association (1899), Western Golf Association (1899), Trans-Mississippi Golf Association (1901), and the Southern Golf Association (1902) were formed. The first ladies golf club was founded at St. Andrews, Scotland, in 1867 and, after the establishment of the Ladies Golf Union in Britain, Lady Margaret Scott won its first tournament. An early dominant female player in the United States was Beatrix Hoyt, who won the second U.S. Women's Amateur, held in 1896.

The game of golf spread throughout the world with significant clubs established in Calcutta (1829) and Bombay (1842) in India; Pau (1856) in France; the Royal Adelaide Golf Club (1870) in Australia; the Royal Cape Golf Club (1885) in South Africa; the Singapore Island Golf Club (1924); and Hirono (1930) in Japan. These courses were designed by architects from the British Isles as part of golf's early manifest destiny. Since then, most countries have developed their own course designers and golf has become a truly international game. This was evident at the 2000 U.S. Open at Pebble Beach when players from South Africa (Ernie Els), Spain (Miguel Angel Jimenez), England (Lee Westwood, Nick Faldo), Ireland (Padraig Harrington), and Fiji (Vijay Singh) were among the top ten finishers.

Among those whom you will meet in this book are the great players such as Horace Hutchinson, Harry Vardon, Tommy Armour, Gene Sarazen, Walter Hagen, Bobby Jones, Joyce Wethered, Glenna Collett, Ben Hogan, Sam Snead, Byron Nelson, Arnold Palmer, Gary Player, Jack Nicklaus, Billy Casper, Mickey Wright, Nancy Lopez, Tom Watson, and Tiger Woods, as well as outstanding teachers, writers, architects, and other contributors such as Bernard Darwin, Herbert Warren Wind, Pete Dye, Harvey Penick, Dan Jenkins, Peggy Kirk Bell, David Leadbetter, Butch Harmon, and many others.

I am hoping that you will find some inspiring thoughts in these pages that add to your imagination and enthusiasm when you tee up and work your way down fairways to come.

CHAPTER 1

GOLF,
THE OBSESSION

Anyone who has played golf knows how easy it is to become obsessed by the game. How easy it is to get lost in the memory of bets won and lost from matches gone by. Or to reminisce about the time you rose before dawn to get a decent tee time or pay an early visit to the practice range, working on that pesky wedge shot that, if mastered, would enable you to break 90. Like he who pursued the mythical white whale, we seek to improve our game—and somehow that perfection is just beyond the horizon. We know it and strive to achieve it.

As J. B. Salmond expressed it in his book *The Story of the R&A:*

> Winter, Spring and Summer,
> Autumn, in their seasons;
> Snow and hoar and sunshine
> With wind, and wave, and rain,
> Tempered my whole being,
> Brought me growth and vigour,
> Bent, and whin, and heather
> To pattern my campaign.

It is a statute and ordinit that in na place of the realme be there usit . . . Golfe or uther sic unprofitabill sportis.

—JAMES IV, TO PARLIAMENT IN EDINBURGH, MAY 16, 1491

The pon'drous club upon the ball
   descends
Involved in dust th' exulting orb
   ascends

—THOMAS MATHISON, *THE GOFF* (1743)

If there be added to its golfing charms the charms of all its surroundings—the grand history of St. Andrews and its sacred memories—its delightful air—the song of its numberless larks, which nestle among the whins—the scream of the sea-birds flying overhead—the blue sea dotted with a few fishing boats— the noise of its waves—the bay of the Eden as seen from the high hole when the tide is full—the venerable towers and the broken outline of the ancient city; and in the distance the Forfarshire Coast, with the range of the Sidlaws, and further off, the Grampian Hills, it may be truly said that, probably no portion of ground of the same size on the whole surface of the globe has afforded so much innocent enjoyment to so many people of all ages from two to eighty-nine, and during so many generations.

—JAMES BALFOUR, *REMINISCENCES OF GOLF
ON ST. ANDREWS LINKS* (1887)

All distinctions of rank were leveled by the joyous spirit of the game. Lords of session and cobblers, knights, baronets and tailors might be seen earnestly contesting for the palm of superior dexterity.

—STATISTICAL ACCOUNT OF SCOTLAND IN THE EIGHTEENTH CENTURY, *THE ENCYCLOPEDIA OF GOLF* (1975)

We saw several elderly citizens playing at the old Scots game of golf, which is a kind of gigantic variety of billiards.

—PETER MORRIS, *PETER'S LETTERS TO HIS KINSFOLK* (1819)

All that is requisite in golf, so it seems to the onlooker, is to hit; and then a "hit," nothing surely can be simpler or easier— so simple and easy that to have a dozen sticks to hit with, and to hire a boy to carry them, is not so much a sign of pitiable insanity as of wilful stupidity.

—ARNOLD HAULTAIN, *THE MYSTERY OF GOLF* (1908)

Golf—a game probably evolved from Dutch antecedents, first recorded in Scotland in the fifteenth century, and played under codified rules since the middle of the eighteenth century; now consisting of hitting a golf ball, using an array of golf clubs by successive strokes into each of nine or eighteen holes on a golf course.

—*THE RULES OF GOLF*, PUBLISHED BY THE ROYAL & ANCIENT GOLF CLUB IN ST. ANDREWS, SCOTLAND, AND THE UNITED STATES GOLF ASSOCIATION

The golf is so long a favourite and peculiar exercise of the Scots is much in use here (Musselburgh). Children are trained to it in their early days, being enticed by the beauty of the links (which lie on each side of the river between the towns and sea), and excited by the example of their parents.

—ANDREW LANG, "THE HISTORY OF GOLF" IN
THE BADMINTON LIBRARY: GOLF (1890)

Golf takes place in "large and glorious places," not on a limited patch of ground. It can be played anywhere: in the mountains; at the seashore; "by the stream and o'er the mead"; through somnolent valleys and over crowded pastureland surrounded by noisy suburban dwellings; and on the silent desert. The extent and form of a golf course lie in the nature of the terrain. You never find two courses exactly alike. Memory enshrines the finest players where we have played golf or seen it played.

—AL LANG, *FOLLOWING THE LEADERS* (1991)

It is not difficult to account for the popularity of the game. It affords, as few other games (if any) do, moderate yet sufficient exercise for all, sufficient for the young and strong, and yet not too violent for those who are older or less robust. While it is simple enough for the unambitious to play with pleasure, it demands, if it is to be played really well, quite as high degree of skill as cricket, tennis or any other first class game. It is a game for players of all degrees and ages; for the veteran of seventy, as for the boy of seven. It cannot be learnt too soon, and it is never too late to begin it.

—LORD WELLWOOD, "GENERAL REMARKS ON THE GAME"
IN *THE BADMINTON LIBRARY: GOLF* (1890)

I am sometimes inclined to think that the high-handicap player gets quite as much, if not more, enjoyment from his golf than does the man who receives only a small number of strokes from scratch. We are not so much depressed when we miss our drive, because it happens to us so much more frequently, and the joy we experience when we execute a perfect shot (and this sometimes does happen) is all the keener because of its comparative rarity.

—BERNARD DARWIN, "PORTRAIT OF A HIGH-HANDICAP GOLFER" IN *THE DARWIN SKETCHBOOK* (WRITINGS FROM 1910 TO 1958)

When, in oratory or in writing, he became rather involved in his metaphors and talked of the soul or the spirit of golf, which perhaps on analysis meant nothing in particular, the utter genuineness of his feeling came through. When he wanted his own way it was apparent that he wanted it for no selfish ends but for the glory of golf.

—BERNARD DARWIN, "CHARLES BLAIR MACDONALD" IN *THE DARWIN SKETCHBOOK* (WRITINGS FROM 1910 TO 1958)

Of course, everyone knows what the news was, because it was the most dramatic story in the history of golf. Ouimet beat Vardon and Ray by five and six shots respectively. He was the first amateur to win the U.S. Open. The details can be found in the record books and old newspaper files. What you cannot find there is the effect of the victory, because, tremendous as it was from a competitive point of view, historically it was even more significant. The cheers from Brookline shook the country.

Ouimet became a national sports hero, and he made America golf-conscious.

—AL LANEY, *FOLLOWING THE LEADERS* (1968)

Golf may be . . . a sophisticated game. At least, it is usually played with the outward appearance of great dignity. It is, nevertheless, a game of considerable passion, either of the explosive type, or that which burns inwardly and sears the soul.

—BOBBY JONES

When golf was over for the day, the bar parlour became the centre for many musical evenings, the singing being conducted by Thomas Owen Potter with Robert (Pendulum) Brown at the piano. This latter gentleman, now the oldest member of the club, was always ready to back himself to play a certain number of strokes by moonlight, a feat, it is said, he often accomplished in fewer strokes than under more normal conditions.

—GUY B. FARRAR, *AROUND GOLF* (1938)

So many of the players of my day were deprived as youngsters. We needed to play. We needed to win. We had lived through several worldwide deprivations—World War I, the Great Depression, World War II. Kids today can't appreciate what it was like to go to bed at night in fear that the world as we knew it might be drastically changed when we woke up in the morning.

—SAM SNEAD, *THE GAME I LOVE* (1997)

A round of golf partakes of the journey, and the journey is one of the central myths and signs of Western man . . . If it is a journey, it is also a round: it always leads back to the place where you started from . . . Golf is always a trip back to the first tee, the more you play the more you realize you are staying where you are. By playing golf you reenact that secret of the journey. You may even get to enjoy it.

—SHIVAS IRONS, IN *GOLF IN THE KINGDOM*
BY MICHAEL MURPHY (1972)

Golf is just one thing to me—the pure pleasure of the golf swing.

—MICKEY WRIGHT, WINNER OF EIGHTY-TWO LPGA TOURNAMENTS

I went to a country school with three grades in one room. The school bus used to pass a golf course, and one day I got them to let me out there. I found out I could make money by caddying on weekends, so I did. I carried two bags and eventually I made more money than my mother, who was working in a department store.

—SANDRA PALMER, LPGA PROFESSIONAL, IN *THE GREAT
WOMEN GOLFERS*, EDITED BY HERBERT WARREN WIND
AND ROBERT MACDONALD (1961)

I would go to school in the morning. Go home for lunch. Then I was supposed to go back to school. But I didn't. I would leave my books in a big pipe that was between my house and the school. I would take my five-iron and go to the beach. Or, if there was no one around, I would sneak onto the far end of the golf course where I couldn't be seen. I'd be there all afternoon.

—SEVE BALLESTEROS, WINNER OF THREE BRITISH OPENS
AND TWO MASTERS, IN *GOLF DIGEST* (2000)

Mac told me he'd gone to the nearest sporting goods store and gotten seventeen Louisville Slugger baseball bats, thirty-four ounces. He'd proceeded to take a Sharpie pen and scribe on the bats the location and date of every qualifying school he'd missed. Then he'd taken those bats, in the dead of night, to a tree in back of the second green at the TPC of Jacksonville, where we had qualified, and broken every one over that pine tree in a primal ceremony. Welcome to the edge.

—GARY MCCORD ON MAC O'GRADY CELEBRATING
WINNING HIS CARD AT THE PGA TOUR QUALIFYING
SCHOOL IN 1983, *JUST A RANGE BALL IN
A BOX OF TITLEISTS* (1997)

My father was the only one in my family who played golf, and he taught me the basics. Then I started taking lessons from Harvey Penick at the Austin Country Club when I was in college at the University of Texas. For my first lesson Harvey charged me three dollars. Even then that wasn't a lot, but Harvey never charged much. Anyway, I stayed out there with him for about an hour and a half. The next time I went to see him, when I got ready to pay he said, "No, I'm just telling you things I told you last week," and he never let me pay him again. I got a lot of mileage out of that first three dollars. I took lessons from Harvey for twenty years. He's the only teacher I've ever had, and I owe a great deal of my success to him, just as Ben Crenshaw, Tom Kite, and a lot of others.

—BETSY RAWLS IN *THE GREAT WOMEN GOLFERS*, EDITED BY HERBERT WARREN WIND AND ROBERT MACDONALD (1961)

Why do I enjoy [golf] after thirty-one years, going out there and doing the things that are necessary to compete—having to practice, having to work, having to dedicate yourself? I guess it comes down to the competition. My personality is such that I'm not going to play if I'm not competitive.

That's the hard thing, the time it takes to keep yourself prepared. That I still have the discipline and the drive to get out there day after day, beat balls and putt and chip, do my hour of stretching and exercise. I really don't understand why I keep doing that. I guess we could go ask Arnold. I guess it's something that is there in you and never goes away.

—RAYMOND FLOYD, IN *GOLF DIGEST* (1994)

Golf is not a fair game. A player can hit a perfect shot and have the ball end up out of bounds, or miss a shot completely and have the ball go in the hole . . . Golf is about how well you accept your misses much more so than it is a game of perfect shots.

—BOB ROTELLA, *365 ANECDOTES AND LESSONS* (1997)

I have a sharp word of sermonizing for the pros of the United States Tour, especially the younger ones. They are getting rich right now on the work of other men, some great ones who, comparatively speaking, never made vast sums from their lifetimes in golf: Walter Hagen, Gene Sarazen, Byron Nelson, Sam Snead, Ben Hogan, Jimmy Demaret. They are the personalities who captivated the public, they made pro golf a successful sport in this country, and they did it when you had a big year if you made ten thousand dollars!

—MARK MCCORMACK, FOUNDER OF INTERNATIONAL MANAGEMENT GROUP, IN *THE GAME I LOVE* BY SAM SNEAD (1997)

I'm blind, but my passion for the game is 20/20.

—A BLIND GOLFER, IN A USGA TELEVISION GOLF PROMOTION DURING THE 2000 U.S. OPEN

The guys who played the day without distinction usually have a certain vague look in their eyes. Kind of like the eyes of an armadillo in your headlights just before becoming road kill. Glazed but aware . . . They're hitting balls twice as fast as the guys who played well. They are not looking around to see who is watching. Their caddies are attentive and have that broken look about them. They are both seeking answers, but do not know the question.

It is the range and all the golfing world resides there.

—GARY MCCORD, PGA TOUR JOURNEYMAN, *JUST A RANGE BALL IN A BOX OF TITLEISTS* (1997)

One's best rounds will forever offer up pleasant memories and the desire to play those courses again to perhaps experience similar joys once more is quite natural. So too, I like to think, is harboring the hope that by having another go at a longtime nemesis, I might somehow expunge the record of some of my darkest moments on the links. Alas, in my case, the latter category offers infinitely more opportunities.

—SWILCAN BURNS, GOLF WRITER AND PGA
TOURNAMENT OFFICIAL (2000)

After all, what leads you on in golf is this. You think a perfect pitch of excellence can be attained. But that pitch of excellence continually recedes the nearer you approach it. Intellectual apprehension outruns physical achievement. Accordingly, the allurement is unceasing, and the fascination endless. Always you can imagine a longer drive, a more accurate approach, a more certain putt; never or rarely ever do you effect all three at every hole on the course. But all men—who are golfers—always live in hope of accomplishing them.

—ARNOLD HAULTAIN, *THE MYSTERY OF GOLF* (1908)

No matter how others try, they don't have the God-given talent like he does. Talent is going to win out in the long haul. What can they do now? Nothing. Work hard, fine. Get in better shape, fine. But you can't outwork him, you can't outcondition him, and they certainly can't outthink him on the golf course. So where is there to improve?

—EARL WOODS ON TIGER WOODS AFTER HIS 67-66-67-69
BRITISH OPEN WIN AT ST. ANDREWS IN 2000

The Scots say that Nature itself dictated that golf should be played by the seashore. Rather, the Scots saw in eroded sea-coasts a cheap battleground on which they could whip their fellow man in a game based on the Calvinist doctrine that man is meant to suffer here below and never more than when he goes out to enjoy himself. The Scots, indeed, ascribe the origins of golf to nothing less than the divine purpose working through geology.

—ALISTAIR COOKE, "THE FINE FLOWER OF MANY LANDSCAPES,"
IN *THE WORLD ATLAS OF GOLF*, EDITED BY
PAT WARD-THOMAS, CARLES PRICE, DONALD STEEL,
AND HERBERT WARREN WIND (1991)

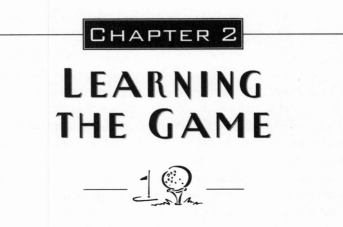

CHAPTER 2

LEARNING THE GAME

Some, like Young Tom Morris, Bobby Jones, Jack Nicklaus, and Tiger Woods, were early golf prodigies. Although they had their struggles, they seem to have had a certain genius for the game. They somehow were able to overcome, or at least stave off, inexorable fate more often than most. The beauty of golf is that it can be played with rudimentary tools. The barriers to entry are low. But to continue to try, as the knowledge and challenge of the game accumulate, takes a strong will and a big heart.

Seve Ballesteros recalls how he learned the game: "I acquired my first golf club at the age of seven, a rustic model made from an old three-iron head, with a stick I cut myself for a shaft. I used pebbles for golf balls."

It is the short game—the approaching and putting—that wins the match. Nevertheless, despite the truth of this, it may be quite safely asserted that if there were no driving there would be very little golf.

—HORACE G. HUTCHINSON, "ELEMENTARY INSTRUCTION: DRIVING" IN *THE BADMINTON LIBRARY: GOLF* (1890)

Why is it that, amongst the thousand-and-one games to-day played by men, women and children in Europe and America, why is it that golf commands so large a share of attention, or serious and thoughtful attention?. . . In the first place, no other game has so simple an object or one requiring, apparently, so simple an exertion of muscular effort. To knock a ball into a hole—that seems the acme of ease.

In the second place, when the novice begins to give some serious consideration to the game, he discovers that there is such a thing as style in golf, and a good style results in good golf . . . In the third place, having progressed a bit, having learned with a certain degree of skill to manipulate his several clubs; having learned also and being able to more or less to put into practice certain carefully conned rules as to how he shall stand and how he shall swing, the beginner . . . discovers that he has not yet learned everything . . . This we may call the social or moral element. It affects the feelings or emotions; it affects the mind through these feelings or emotions; and, through the mind it affects the muscles.

—ARNOLD HAULTAIN, *THE MYSTERY OF GOLF* (1908)

A sound preshot routine is the rod and staff of the golfer under pressure, a comfort in times of affliction and challenge. It ensures that he sets up properly, physically and mentally. It blocks out distractions. It helps him to produce his best golf under pressure.

—BOB ROTELLA, *GOLF IS NOT A GAME OF PERFECT* (1995)

The four fundamentals of good golf form, according to Sargent, are:

1. The steady head
2. Proficiency in handling the club
3. The straight left arm
4. The close-in right elbow

That's all the golf shotmaking technique you need to know, according to the way Sargent, a very successful teacher, looked at the game.

—HERB GRAFFIS ABOUT GEORGE SARGENT,
ESQUIRE'S WORLD OF GOLF (1965)

Genius has been defined as an infinite capacity for taking pains; and, be that how it may as a definition of universal genius, it is a most happy definition of golfing genius . . . But yet you must not cultivate this infinite carefulness to the loss of freedom. The learner who consistently misses the ball in a good free style is a golfing infant of more promise than one who confidently hits a certain wretched distance in a stiff and cramped style; albeit for the time being the latter will always defeat the former. Do not be so scientific as to lose all dash.

—HORACE HUTCHINSON, *HINTS ON THE GAME OF GOLF* (1886)

Do not get in the habit of counting strokes from the beginning of the round in every match that you play, in the hope that each time you may be able to beat your own record for the course. If you do so, and play one or two bad holes to begin with, you will suffer from a sense of disappointment which may have a bad effect upon your play for the remainder of the game.

—HARRY VARDON, *THE COMPLETE GOLFER* (1905)

You will find that the more you get into the habit of making the vagaries of your surroundings an excuse for a bad stroke, the more real and powerful will their distracting influence become. If you can bring yourself to treat those trifling distractions, even when they have put you off your stroke, with the silent contempt they merit, you will soon grow to disregard them—whereby you will become a better golfer, and pleasanter.

—HORACE HUTCHINSON,
HINTS ON THE GAME OF GOLF (1886)

A golfer's education is never finished; he certainly may forget a little of what he has learnt, but he can always pick up some simple wrinkle which may be of use to him in his other career . . .

In every walk of life a child or a man has ambitions; without them he is of little use to this world. My ambition has always been to conquer something in the game of golf.

—HAROLD HILTON, *MY GOLFING REMINISCENCES* (1907)

No man should attempt to play golf who has not good legs to run with and good arms to throw with, as well as a modicum of brain power to direct his play. It is also, by the nature of the game itself, a most aristocratic exercise, for no man can play at golf who has not a servant at hand to assist him. It is possible that no sport exists in which the services of a paid assistant are so essential as in this national game of Scotland.

—FROM AN ARTICLE IN THE *PHILADELPHIA TIMES*,
FEBRUARY 24, 1889

Francis Ouimet affords as good an illustration as anyone can want of the American golfing temperament, which is, by the way, often misunderstood by English golfers. He is, or at any rate used to be, intensely keen; he can work at the game like a slave and fight like a hero, but he has the national genius for "letting up" between battles, and there is no more cheerful and amusing person in all the championship field.

—BERNARD DARWIN, "FRANCIS" IN *THE DARWIN SKETCHBOOK*
(WRITINGS FROM 1910 TO 1958)

He would tolerate no deviation from the correct path, even in a friendly round. In the early days of the game, when there was an even greater laxity in playing the rules than anyone can know today, he set a standard which gradually took effect . . . he never played a careless, indifferent shot. No matter how unimportant the match, he played every stroke as if he were in a championship test. He made careful, accurate golf a habit.

—GRANTLAND RICE ON THE STYLE OF WALTER TRAVIS,
"THE OLD MAN" IN *THE AMERICAN GOLFER* MAGAZINE (1922)

The smaller the target, the sharper the athlete's focus, the better his concentration, and the better the results . . . The small, precise target helps golfers in one obvious way, by making it easier to align the player and his club. But it has another benefit. A golfer needs to have something on his mind if he does not want thoughts about swing mechanics to intrude on his consciousness just as he is preparing to play his shot. The target helps fill that void. It helps prevent distractions.

—BOB ROTELLA, *GOLF IS NOT A GAME OF PERFECT* (1995)

I never hurried, there was no use worrying—and I always took time to smell the roses along the way.

—WALTER HAGEN, *THE WALTER HAGEN STORY* (1956)

In his most youthful and tempestuous days he had never been angry with his opponent and not often, I think, with Fate, but he had been furiously angry with himself. He set himself an almost impossibly high standard, he thought it an act of incredible folly if not positive crime to make a stroke, that was not exactly as it ought to be made. If he ever derogated from that standard he may even in his most mature days, have been "mad" in the recesses of his heart, but he became outwardly a man of ice, with the very best of golfing manners.

—BERNARD DARWIN ON BOBBY JONES, "THE GREATEST OF THEM ALL" IN *THE DARWIN SKETCHBOOK* (WRITINGS FROM 1910 TO 1958)

If you want to cultivate a real fault, try to swing without swaying the hips or twisting them. If you can get to doing that—then you'll have a fine case for the golf doctor. That's one of the first things a beginner tries to do. After you get him impressed with the idea that he mustn't sway his whole body back and forth, he almost always tries to get the club back with arms alone. That's a whale of a fault.

—STEWART MAIDEN TO O. B. KEELER, "THE MOST COMMON FAULTS" IN *THE AMERICAN GOLFER* MAGAZINE (1922)

The swing is a completely left-handed swing, with the right entering only at the bottom to give the speed and power the left or back-handed stroke lacks . . . About the time you feel the club head progressing at an easy, uniform speed near your right hip, without quickening, without tightening, push your right hand evenly and smoothly right toward the hole. Don't quit until the swing is completely finished.

Your right hand has not entered into the swing at all until the club enters the speed section. The thought is not one of effort but to support the weaker left hand and keep the club head from lagging behind. The pushing right hand prevents it, and speed comes without effort . . .

—EDDIE LOOS, "THE ROLE OF THE LEFT HAND: A CLEAR
AND COMPREHENSIVE ANALYSIS OF ITS FUNCTION"
IN *THE AMERICAN GOLFER* MAGAZINE (1925)

I suddenly realized that golf is simply a game of targets. Each shot should be played with some definite objective in mind.

Any definite objective is a target. Therefore, every shot in golf should be played as a shot at some clearly defined target. All players realize this when they are playing a shot to the green. A narrow opening between bunkers, or the pin itself, may be the target. But what many of them forget is that the shot off the tee should, also, be aimed at some target down the fairway.

Too many players—and I was one of them—seek only to gain distance off the tee. They think that as long as they belt on out from 225 to 275 yards, depending on the average distance gained by the individual, and providing that the drive stays on the fairway, the tee shot has been a success. That is not true. The tee shot is not a perfect shot unless it is so placed as to open up the hole for the second shot.

—CRAIG WOOD, IN "CRAIG WOOD TELLS HOW HE DID IT"
BY MAXWELL STYLES IN *THE AMERICAN GOLFER* MAGAZINE (1933)

I learned by copying. My father used to take Roger and me to watch golf when we were youngsters, and I tried to copy the good players' rhythm. Then, when I began playing fairly well, I played a lot with Roger and his friends from Oxford.

—JOYCE WETHERED, IN "HIGH TEE" BY RICHARD F. MILLER
IN *TOWN & COUNTRY* MAGAZINE (1977)

This is the first mental principle a golfer must learn. A person with great dreams can achieve great things. A person with small dreams, or a person without the confidence to pursue his or her dreams, has consigned himself or herself to a life of frustration and mediocrity.

—BOB ROTELLA, *GOLF IS NOT A GAME OF PERFECT* (1995)

In order to develop a golf swing your thoughts must run in the right direction. Otherwise it will be impossible. Perhaps you will understand me better when I say that when you grip a golf club to take your first swing at a golf ball every natural instinct you employ to accomplish that objective is wrong, absolutely wrong.

—BEN HOGAN, *BEN HOGAN'S POWER GOLF* (1948)

When a child shows interest, and if there is some ability there, then that kid—on his or her own—will want to get at somebody he or she can play against. That's the whole thing, I think: Get children into the right level of competition as early as they can handle it. When talented youngsters don't have a chance to play with other kids of similar ability, then the danger is that they will lose interest in the game because they won't be able to tell how good they really are . . .

—SAM SNEAD, *THE GAME I LOVE* (1997)

Youngsters tend to emulate the players, and if they see us
playing matches with one club, they'll start doing it, too.
And that's really the best way to learn to play the game.
If you're allowed only one club you will have to create
a tremendous number of different shots with it. It's the
best way for youngsters to learn finesse on the course
and to develop a tremendous feel around the greens.

—LEE TREVINO, *THE SNAKE IN THE SAND TRAP AND*
OTHER MISADVENTURES ON THE GOLF TOUR (1985)

When pros talk together about their instruction problems,
almost invariably they refer to the first and most important step
in teaching as that of getting the pupil to relax.

"Why is relaxation so vital?" It has a lot to do with the basic
principal of the method I'll give you for learning good golf.

Why do you grit your teeth, hunch your shoulders, get tense
and taut when you expect pain? The reason is that you thus
hope to deaden your sensibility to the feeling of pain. When you
are relaxed you believe that you'll feel too acutely. Delicacy of
feeling is what we want in golf; hence the high value pros place
on relaxation.

—BEN HOGAN, IN *ESQUIRE'S WORLD OF GOLF*
BY HERB GRAFFIS (1965)

I was a hothead, but I got it taken out of me real fast. I was the
first one ever to get a fine on the tour. I paid $150 for smarting
off to a sponsor. I was young and righteous. But you cannot
become a champion without developing the ability to cope with
your emotions. That's the most important factor in becoming a
winner. This is what it's all about—being able to control every

emotion: elation, dejection, fear, greed, the whole lot. I see girls who can overcome anger. They learn not to get mad when they hit a poor shot. But they still go bananas with joy when they make a good putt. You have to control the whole thing. It takes a tremendous amount of energy, because it's not natural.

—Mickey Wright to Kathy Jonah, in *Golf Digest* (1976)

Golf can be a source of relief from tension and stress; it can also be a severe test of one's emotional control. Your two emotions most commonly displayed in the game are anger and fear. Ability to cope with these two emotions will certainly affect your success and enjoyment in golf.

—Gary Wiren, *Golf* (1971)

When I was three, my father put my hands in his and placed them around the shaft of a cut-down women's golf club. He showed me the classic overlap, or Vardon grip—the proper grip for a good golf swing, he said—and told me to hit the golf ball . . . "Hit it hard boy. Go find it and hit it again."

—Arnold Palmer, *A Golfer's Life*
with James Dodson (1999)

The next day he started telling the guys in the pro shop, in front of me, about how I played nine holes in even par for the first time in my life. I felt sick. I never lied about my score again in my life. I never lied to my father again. I didn't know then what I'm sure of now: Of course Dad knew I hadn't shot 36 for nine holes. If I had, I would have sprinted from the ninth green all the way home to tell him the news, and he knew it. I think another father might have said, "Are you telling me the truth about that score?" There's nothing wrong with that. My father's approach though, was different. His lesson took quickly and will stay forever.

—DAVIS LOVE III, IN *CHICKEN SOUP FOR THE GOLFER'S SOUL*, EDITED BY JACK CANFIELD, MARK VICTOR HANSEN, JEFF AUBREY, MARK DONNELLY, AND CHRISSY DONNELLY (1999)

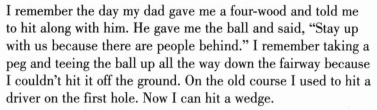

I remember the day my dad gave me a four-wood and told me to hit along with him. He gave me the ball and said, "Stay up with us because there are people behind." I remember taking a peg and teeing the ball up all the way down the fairway because I couldn't hit it off the ground. On the old course I used to hit a driver on the first hole. Now I can hit a wedge.

—NANCY LOPEZ TO GRACE LICHTENSTEIN, IN *THE NEW YORK TIMES MAGAZINE* (1978)

When someone decides to seriously learn the game, I first find out their expectations. Once that is determined, I advise learners not to try to improve too quickly. It takes time and work even to achieve minimum ability in golf, especially if you are an older learner. Don't raise your expectations too high. It is easy to get discouraged in this game. Most of all, have fun and enjoy it. One thing that I have noticed, more and more young people are taking up the game, largely due to exciting new players such as Tiger Woods and Sergio Garcia.

—TOM SMACK, DIRECTOR OF GOLF AND HEAD PROFESSIONAL, THE SAGAMORE GOLF CLUB, BOLTON LANDING, NEW YORK (2000)

The more mechanical you become in making these preparations before you swing, the greater your chances for success. Therefore, try to develop a routine which you can automatically follow in the course of getting ready to hit a golf shot.

1. Approach your shot from behind your line to the pin so you can visualize where you want to aim.
2. Decide upon the selection of your club and how strongly you intend to hit with it.
3. Take a careful and uniform grip.
4. Sole the club head behind the ball, placing the bottom line of the club face at right angles to your line of flight.
5. Draw an imaginary line, perpendicular to your line of flight, which runs from the club head to the correct position between your feet for the placement of the ball for that particular club.
6. Place first your left foot, then your right, into a position that is comfortable and correct for the club, and keep the club head square to the target.
7. Make your swing.

—GARY WIREN, *GOLF* (1971)

Lessons are important in golf because it is easier to create a good habit than to change a bad one. Older golfers tend to be set in their ways while youngsters just starting out can adapt more quickly. It is important to start with the right fundamentals. Here at Buffalo Dunes we have 160 junior golfers in our summer program. They are given a one-hour tee lesson and then they play three, six, nine, or eighteen holes depending on their stage of development. I let beginning students take a score card out onto the golf course but I don't give them a pencil to

keep score. I advise them to stay in the present and to play one
shot at a time.

—PAUL PARKER, HEAD PROFESSIONAL, BUFFALO DUNES GOLF
COURSE, GARDEN CITY, KANSAS (2000)

That you are a very indifferent player is no reason that you
should be placed in a position from which you are likely to win
every prize for which you enter. Golf is not charity.

—HORACE HUTCHINSON, *HINTS ON THE GAME OF GOLF* (1886)

I don't think you're ever finished trying to improve. As soon
as you feel like you're finished, then I guess you are finished,
because you've already put a limit on what you can attain.
I don't think that's right.

—TIGER WOODS, IN *GOLFWEEK* (1999)

How you learn the game can depend on your budget. I learned
by playing with better players at my local club. I watched them
and copied their best characteristics. Some people learn by tape
recording professional tournaments then analyzing and imitating
the swings of players on the PGA and LPGA Tour. Others get
tips from the Golf Channel, magazines, instructional videos,
books, and other instructional materials. And, of course, you
can take private lessons. Instruction over the Internet is here
now that broadband high-speed video is available. The golfer
can transmit a video of his or her swing to an online service and
then receive personalized swing analysis from leading instructors online. I am involved in a project called modelgolf.com

as part of Compusport that has developed computer models of the "ideal" golf swing based on a composite of swings of leading golfers. We will use many of the swing analysis and instructional techniques online that we have developed here at Grand Cypress.

—FRED GRIFFEN, DIRECTOR OF THE GRAND CYPRESS
GOLF ACADEMY, ORLANDO, FLORIDA (2000)

I've found that, although many new players are coming into the game, many drop out quickly because they have unrealistic expectations and have not been taught properly. For example, some kids just want to hit the ball far, and if they can't, they get frustrated and give up. It takes more than hitting the ball far to play golf.

—MARIAN BURKE BLAIN, HEAD PROFESSIONAL,
SEVEN OAKS, COLGATE UNIVERSITY,
HAMILTON, NEW YORK (2000)

Set up goals for yourself before each round and keep them simple. Pick one or two aspects to try to improve on—say you won't have any three-putts, or you'll hit ten fairways instead of eight in your round. Or, if you shoot a 45, on the front, go for a 44 on the back. Little goals add up to big achievements—like lower scores.

—HELEN ALFREDSSON, "PLAY YOUR 'A' GAME"
IN *GOLF FOR WOMEN* MAGAZINE (2000)

Women are generally more comfortable learning in groups. New-comers to the game can find it daunting having a professional standing over them for thirty minutes or an hour. It helps to remember that everybody misses the ball repeatedly in their first two or three lessons. If you are having a lesson on your own, you might imagine that you are the first person your professional has ever seen miss the ball! You can really feel stupid. In a group lesson, however, what is daunting on your own can be fun. You realize that everyone else has the same problems.

—VIVIEN SAUNDERS, *THE GOLF HANDBOOK FOR WOMEN* (2000)

Golf is unique among games because so often you are the judge as to whether you've broken a rule or not. The rules put you on your honor to call a violation on yourself.

I was playing in a college event called the Beehive Invitational. I was leading the tournament and came to this par-3, where I hit my ball into a long rut just short of the green. I went up to the ball, knocked it stiff, and tapped it into the hole. When I picked the ball out of the hole, I saw that it was the wrong ball—it wasn't my ball. Now, nobody knew it was the wrong ball but me. It would have been very, very easy for me to just go ahead and say nothing.

I told the guys I was playing with what had happened and we went back and found my ball. I ended up taking a two-stroke penalty and played out the hole with my own ball. The story did have a happy ending, though. I did win the tournament.

—JOHNNY MILLER, *JOHNNY MILLER'S GOLF FOR JUNIORS: BASIC PRINCIPLES OF THE GAME* WITH DESMOND TOLHURST (1987)

CHAPTER 3

THE GRIP

Many golf experts contend that the grip is the key to proper swing mechanics. There have been the baseball grip, the overlapping grip, the interlocking grip, and others. Golf instructors relate that the hands are the golfer's only connection with the club, therefore making it vital that they be placed on the grip of the club correctly. And pros will often tell you that a neutral grip, with both Vs of the hands (formed by the index fingers and thumbs), should point to the right ear at address.

Gene Sarazen once commented: "If I was tutoring a young player, I would instill in him the importance of the grip. If he hasn't got a good grip, he's got two chances: slim and none."

You can't strangle the club with a hog killer's grip. You've got to hold it as if it were a little bird—gently but firmly. You don't want it to fly away, but you don't want to suffocate the poor thing either. Proper grip pressure that stays consistent throughout the swing enables you to swing more consistently.

—SAM SNEAD, *THE GAME I LOVE* (1997)

Certain points may be noted about the grip, but it is a mistake in striving after a prescribed fashion to work the hands in a position of discomfort. In the first place, a few inches of the shaft should be allowed to project above the left hand, for thus a greater command over the club is acquired. Secondly, since . . . the club has to turn in the right hand at a certain point in the swing, it should be held lightly, in the fingers, rather than in the palm, with that hand. In the left hand it should be held well home in the palm, and it is not to stir from this position throughout the swing. It is the left hand, mainly, that communicated the power of the swing; the chief function of the right hand is a guide in direction. The back of the left hand should be turned towards the direction in which it is intended to drive the ball—turned upwards rather than downwards; for if at all turned downwards, it is almost impossible, as anyone may at once see for himself, to swing the club back round the head without shifting the grip.

—HORACE HUTCHINSON, "ELEMENTARY INSTRUCTION: DRIVING" IN *THE BADMINTON LIBRARY: GOLF* (1890)

The old fixed grip already was being questioned. Several of the thoughtful amateurs at St. Andrews were using the overlapping grip that eventually was popularized by Vardon and often is identified by his name. The grip is now used by almost all better golfers . . .

The reason for adopting the overlapping grip was that it kept the Vardon hands close together. Vardon held the club principally with his fingers instead of the old-fashioned palm grip which had both thumbs around the shaft and the thumbs and first fingers showing two Vs over the center of the top of the shaft.

Vardon, by the way, was the first great golfer to have in his tactics controlled hooks and slices. That ability was valuable on the wind-swept British seaside courses.

—HERB GRAFFIS, *ESQUIRE'S WORLD OF GOLF* (1965)

I grip quite as firmly with the right hand as with the other one. When the other way is adopted, the left hand being tight and the right hand simply watching it, there is an irresistible tendency for the latter to tighten up suddenly at some part of the upward or downward swing, and, as surely as there is a ball on the tee, when it does so there is mischief. Depend upon it, the instinct of activity will prevent the right hand from going through with the swing in that indefinite state of looseness. Perhaps a yard from the ball in the upward swing, or a yard from it when coming down, there will be a convulsive grip on the right hand, which, with an immediate acknowledgment of guilt, will relax again. Such a happening is usually fatal; it deserves to be. Slicing, pulling, sclaffing, and the foundering of the ball—all these disasters may at times be traced to this determination of the right hand not to be ignored but to have its part to play in the making of the drive. Therefore, in all respects my right hand is a joint partner with the left.

—HARRY VARDON, IN *ESQUIRE'S WORLD OF GOLF*
BY HERB GRAFFIS (1965)

Now relax both hands and let them return to the original position on the club. This tightening and the relaxation will show you the difference between a firm hold and a light hold. In holding the handle properly throughout the entire swing the light hold

should be used. You should hold the club as lightly as though
you were holding a little bird in your hands. You would not
crush it yet you would not want it to fly away.

—PHIL GALVANO, "STARTING YOUR SWING" IN *SECRETS
OF THE GOLFING GREATS*, EDITED BY TOM SCOTT (1965)

A good tip is to keep the little finger of the left hand from being
loosened; then the next two fingers will stay firm. When fingers
of the left hand are closed properly to the grip, these are the
firm points of pressure you feel . . .

The grip with both hands—the V of the right thumb and
forefinger also points to your right shoulder. Forefinger of right
hand is against the side of shaft in strongest position for hit.
Hands fitted compactly together. Pressure of right-hand grip
one-half that of the left-hand grip.

—TOMMY ARMOUR, *HOW TO PLAY YOUR
BEST GOLF ALL THE TIME* (1953)

Now there are so many different ways of holding a golf club.
Practically every first-class golfer grips the club in the manner
slightly different from every other. For instance there is the ordinary two-handed grip used by Abe Mitchell and Sandy Herd.
Then there is the overlapping grip popularized by Vardon and
Taylor; also the interlocking grip so successfully used by Francis
Ouimet and Sarazen. The question of which one to use must be
left to the individual, but whatever grip is adopted, one thing must
not be lost sight of; and that is golf is a two-handed game, and one
must help the other to get as much to the club head as possible.

—ERNEST JONES, "SWING THE CLUBHEAD: A PLEA FOR
SIMPLICITY IN ANALYZING THE GOLF SWING" IN
THE AMERICAN GOLFER MAGAZINE (1927)

The most serious and most frequent deviation of the club face from its proper position occurs at the top of the swing. The big idea—the essential one—is to hold the club at address with easy security rather than grim, tightening intensity.

Golf is a game to be played with two hands. Your left hand guides the club and keeps the face in the desired position for the hit, and the power pours through the coupling of the right hand and the club. Always have your mind made up that you are going to whip your right hand into the shot. That is a "must."

—TOMMY ARMOUR, *HOW TO PLAY YOUR BEST GOLF ALL THE TIME* (1953)

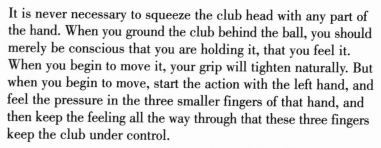

It is never necessary to squeeze the club head with any part of the hand. When you ground the club behind the ball, you should merely be conscious that you are holding it, that you feel it. When you begin to move it, your grip will tighten naturally. But when you begin to move, start the action with the left hand, and feel the pressure in the three smaller fingers of that hand, and then keep the feeling all the way through that these three fingers keep the club under control.

—BOBBY JONES, "USING YOUR HANDS" IN *THE AMERICAN GOLFER* MAGAZINE (1934)

Tommy Armour recommends what he calls a trigger grip with the forefinger of the right hand hooked onto the shaft and the thumb a little to the left of the shaft. This sets up the grip for a lively lash with the right hand. Armour says that the largest third of the forefinger performs an important function in working on the shaft so it whips the club into the shot. He also recommends that the sensitive touch of the tips of the forefinger and thumb provide feeling essential to a controlled long shot.

—HERB GRAFFIS, *ESQUIRE'S WORLD OF GOLF* (1965)

Here is the most serious frequent error at the top of the swing—loosening the left hand grip. That compels you to make the mistake of starting to hit from the top of the swing and to hit with the body instead of the hands. Then anything can happen—slicing, hooking, topping, hitting under the ball, or missing it altogether.

—TOMMY ARMOUR, *HOW TO PLAY YOUR BEST GOLF ALL THE TIME* (1953)

Those who reverse this order, maintaining a firm grip with the right hand, a flabby hold with the left—and this is not at all uncommon among beginners who are accustomed to playing right-handed games—these will lift the club to the shoulder instead of swinging it back. None will obtain a sufficient turn of the hips and shoulders, and the position at the top of the swing, with both arms bent, will be wholly lacking in poise. The impression is that such a player, if he hits the ball at all, will do so only because of the kindness of fortune.

—BOBBY JONES, *BOBBY JONES ON GOLF* (1966)

Her hands are the weakest part of a woman golfer. Watching long handicap players, it is rare to see them holding the club correctly. Few reach the top of their swing without slackening their grasp, nor do they regain it before the head of the club makes contact with the ball. There are several explanations for this but the common cause is lack of strength in the fingers and hands . . .

Miss [Ruth] Porter realized that she needed more length in order to go places in senior golf. She started working on her hands, squeezing a squash ball, rolling up newspapers and wringing pieces of cloth.

—ENID WILSON, *A GALLERY OF WOMEN GOLFERS* (1961)

My theory of the grip differs somewhat from that of many teachers. My grip on the club is designed for firmness, above all else. This is one of the real secrets of hitting a golf ball well. I grip the club very firmly in both hands with the left hand grasping the tighter of the two.

I use what is called the "overlapping" grip. I believe this provides a maximum of coordination between hands. The effect is to make them work as one.

—BYRON NELSON, *BYRON NELSON'S WINNING GOLF* (1946)

It is only through complete coordination of the hands that you can transmit the full power of your body to the club head . . . The overlapping grip to my mind makes the hands work together more than any other.

Keep in mind that the club is not held in the fingers of the left hand but is boxed inside the fist with pressure exerted by the little finger. The club thus rests diagonally across the hand. The V formed by the left thumb and forefinger points directly over the right shoulder . . . Keep that little finger of the left hand tightly closed throughout, and particularly at the top of the backswing!

The grip with the right hand is a complete finger grip. The grip is with the thumb and first three fingers of the right hand, snugged up close to the left hand, with the little finger of the right hand overlapping the left forefinger.

The V formed by the thumb and forefinger of the right hand should be parallel to the V formed by the left thumb and forefinger . . . When the left hand is placed properly, two knuckles are plainly visible on that hand. All you see of the right hand is the thumb and the forefinger.

—SAM SNEAD, *SAM SNEAD'S BASIC GUIDE TO GOOD GOLF* (1961)

In putting and in delicate iron strokes, more use is to be made of the fingers than in strokes which require the full swing. Remember to bring your hands well to the front, nearly opposite the left thigh, when "addressing yourself, as it is called, to the ball."

The preliminary waggle . . . is necessary for acquiring the requisite freedom and play of wrist.

—HORACE HUTCHINSON, *HINTS ON THE GAME OF GOLF* (1886)

Armour . . . employs the orthodox Vardon grip—the little finger of the left, but it is the alignment of the hands on the grip that is unusual. Armour's two hands are well over the top of the shaft. They work in perfect rhythm, these two big hands, attached to unusually powerful wrists . . .

Armour plays a symphony with the irons—backed by this unusually high grip which puts the burden of the weight of the club well down on the palm of the left hand and permits free play and use of the fingers. It is purely a finger grip, this grasp of the club by the master of irons. Nothing else to it. If Tommy permitted his club to slide back in the palm, all the delicacy of touch and hit would be lost, the rhythm destroyed and the efficiency lost.

—WALTER R. McCALLUM, "HOW ARMOUR DOES IT: THE SECRETS
OF HIS SUPERB SKILL AND HOW HE ACQUIRED THEM"
IN *THE AMERICAN GOLFER* MAGAZINE (1927)

If you stop to consider the part of your hands that are used to get a sense of touch from, it will soon be realized that the forefinger and thumb are the principal factors . . .

This is very often the case in gripping the club. The grip from the back of the hand puts the forefinger and thumb out of action, so that great care should be taken to see the club is held in such a manner that the forefinger and thumb are used to the best advantage. A good guide is to see that the tip of the thumb is in line with the second joint of the first finger.

—ERNEST JONES, "SWING THE CLUBHEAD:
A PLEA FOR SIMPLICITY IN THE GOLF SWING"
IN *THE AMERICAN GOLFER* MAGAZINE (1927)

One reason why the grip is so important is because by means of it we telegraph our energy and our desires to the club. To do this with a maximum amount of efficiency we've got to have a grip which will permit our hands and wrists to work properly as one unit and not against each other . . .

In the conventional overlapping grip the little finger of the right hand overlaps the index finger of the left hand, whereas I have found that I am able to get a firmer grip, transmitting more power to the club head, by gripping the little finger of my right hand around the knob of the knuckle of the index finger of my left hand.

—BEN HOGAN, *BEN HOGAN'S POWER GOLF* (1948)

To hook the ball turn both hands toward the right side. It will feel unnatural, but it will enable you to hook without altering your swing. Your hands come back to a normal position while you swing and automatically close the face of the club at impact, insuring a hook.

[To fade the ball] . . . I have turned the hands over toward the left over the shaft. During the swing they come back to a normal position, automatically opening the face of the club and giving the desired fade or slice. In assuming any grip the club face should be square to the line of flight. When gripping the club to play a slice or hook be sure to loosen your hands and regrip, placing them in the desired position.

—BEN HOGAN, *BEN HOGAN'S POWER GOLF* (1948)

I never play a shot without first glancing at my hands. What I check before address is the alignment of the grip with the face of the club. They go together . . . If you have ever watched Jimmy DeMaret, you have no doubt seen him affix his grip, raising the club until his hands are only a foot or so in front of his eyes. Then Jimmy sights down the shaft and checks both his hands and the club head as one unit . . . Gripping a club, you see, is like aiming a rifle. If your hands are improperly aligned with the club head, you will hit only a few isolated accurate shots.

—CLAUDE HARMON, "CHECKING THE GRIP WITH THE CLUB HEAD" IN *TIPS FROM THE TOP*, EDITED BY HERBERT WARREN WIND (1955)

It is truly amazing how greatly an almost imperceptible change in a golfer's grip can alter his swing. I find that when I grip with my hands turned too far to my right I have a tendency to sway my body laterally to the right on my backswing. If my hands are turned too far to the left, I seem to raise my body on the backswing. Obviously swaying and raising the body during the backswing will destroy a player's sense of balance.

—ARNOLD PALMER, *THE ARNOLD PALMER METHOD* (1959)

A prime cause of slicing among all golfers is a subconscious or involuntary tightening of the grip at some point during the swing. The right hand is generally the biggest culprit, grabbing the club so tightly that the wrists cannot release freely and fully through impact. The result is at least an open club face. At worst, there is both an open club face and an out-to-in swing path as a result of the right shoulder being pulled forward by rigid wrists. The cure lies in maintaining an overly firm grip pressure throughout the swing.

—JACK NICKLAUS, *JACK NICKLAUS' LESSON TEE* WITH KEN BOWDEN (1972)

The only link of communication that you have with the golf club is your hands. Proper hand positioning, then, becomes a vital key in the whole process of a golf shot. It is extremely important to develop a good grip immediately so that your line of communications is correctly established. Find a fundamentally sound position to begin with, and stick to it!

—GARY WIREN, *GOLF* (1971)

On the PGA Tour, there are three different types of grip, and one of these should work for you. The weak grip is when the Vs of both hands are pointing right at your nose. A neutral grip is where the Vs are pointed about at your right ear. And then a strong grip is where the Vs are pointing at the right shoulder blade. On tour, each grip really causes a different kind of swing. You'll notice with the strong grip, guys like Azinger and Trevino have a lot of slide and knee action. The neutral grip allows you to get a little bit of slide, but a nice turn also. The weaker grip usually causes a guy to get a lot of hand action at the bottom.

—JOHNNY MILLER (1998)

If you have a bad grip, you don't want a good swing. With a bad grip you have to make unattractive adjustments in your swing to hit the ball squarely . . . I believe it is a nice idea to try to pattern your swing after that of a professional player who is close to your own height and body structure, but only if you also study and imitate that player's grip . . . One grip does not fit all.

—HARVEY PENICK, *HARVEY PENICK'S LITTLE RED BOOK* WITH BUD SHRAKE (1992)

When I face a trouble shot where I have to slice or hook the ball a lot, I will change my grip. Actually it's probably the easiest way for most players to stop slicing and start to hook the ball. And changing your grip in practice is an excellent way to learn about spin and train yourself in trouble shots. To hit a major slice, rotate your hands counterclockwise on the grip. To hit a large hook, rotate your hands clockwise. Do not rotate the club head as you rotate your hands . . .

—TOM WATSON, *TOM WATSON'S STRATEGIC GOLF* WITH NICK SEITZ (1993)

Your golf grip should do two things and two things only:

1. Provide a stable hold on the club through the entire motion, yet allow the free hinging of wrists and arms.
2. Be comfortable.

I use an overlap-style grip in which (for the right-handed player) all fingers of the left hand are placed on the grip. My left hand is turned a shade clockwise on the handle so that my left thumb is positioned just to the right of the top center of the handle. Thus the back of my left hand does not point directly at the target but faces somewhat upward as well . . . I place my right hand on the club so that its palm is square or flush with my left hand . . . The three middle fingers of my right hand close around the grip, while my right little finger overlaps the index finger of my left hand. My right palm then closes over my left thumb . . .

This overlapping position helps wed the two hands securely together throughout the swing. Also, the closer the hands are together in the grip, the more speed you'll generate in the swing.

—FRED COUPLES, *TOTAL SHOTMAKING* (1994)

Grip it parallel: Your hands should work as a single unit to control the club face. Regardless of whether your grip is "strong" (both hands turned more to the right) or "weak" (hands to the left), your hands should be parallel to one another. Check this by holding the club in front of you at eye level. The creases formed by each thumb and forefinger should be parallel. If you tend to slice, turn the lines a bit to your right. If you hook, turn them to your left.

—DAVID LEADBETTER, "HIT IT FARTHER, STRAIGHTER, CLOSER" IN *GOLF DIGEST* (2000)

The grip is one of the most important things I'll teach even a good player. Because this is the only communication you have with the club. Your hands tell the club what to do. If your hands are correctly placed on the club, the swing will be easier. And the correct grip leads to a correct posture over the ball. For example, you are likely to be tilted correctly at address when the club is gripped with your fingers, not back in the pad of your palm. A good grip takes a lot of feel. And it's hard to change a bad grip. Don't let results get in the way of changing your grip. You're going to hit some funky shots at first while correcting your grip. But even Tiger Woods went through one year of swing change to get to the level he is today. You can always improve.

—PAUL PARKER, HEAD GOLF PROFESSIONAL,
BUFFALO DUNES GOLF COURSE,
GARDEN CITY, KANSAS (2000)

CHAPTER 4

THE STANCE

As with all aspects of golf, much has been written about the stance and address. Some of the typical guidelines include: Go through the same preshot ritual every time; take a relaxed position, making certain you are aiming in the proper direction; be sure the ball is properly positioned in your stance, depending on the situation and the club you are using; and use the waggle to keep your hands, wrists, arms, and shoulders from tightening up.

Byron Nelson offers this advice:

> Never reach for the ball. Your weight as you address the ball should be distributed evenly between the ball and heel of each foot, with special emphasis on the left foot. This gives you the best possible foundation for your swing. If you start reaching perceptibly for the ball, the arc of your swing will become too flat. The prominent fault is standing too far from the ball, rather than too close to it. It is next to impossible to stand too close to the ball.

Take dead aim.

—HARVEY PENICK, *HARVEY PENICK'S LITTLE RED BOOK*
WITH BUD SHRAKE (1992)

In addressing the ball, the weight of the body should rest mainly on the left leg. As the club comes back the weight is naturally transferred to the right leg, but should again be thrown forward upon the left as soon as the club head descends and approaches the ball.

Let your arms be free from the body, and bent at an easy natural angle—not tucked in to the sides in the fashion of a trussed fowl, nor stuck out square like the forelegs of a Dachshund, nor, again, stiff and straight in front of you like the arms of a man meditating a dive into water. The left elbow, which will naturally be more bent than the right, since the left hand being uppermost will be near to the shoulder, should be kept sufficiently to the front to swing clear of the body.

—HORACE HUTCHINSON, *HINTS ON THE GAME OF GOLF* (1886)

Those waggles of his, too—they amount as a rule to anything between eight and thirteen—seem to be part of the character of the man. With most of us, a plethora of waggles is a sign of irresolution; in Sandy's case they bespeak the intensest resolution. He has found he cannot get perfectly comfortable and ready to hit the ball without them, and, that being so, no self-consciousness, no knowledge of the smiles of the onlookers, in short no power on earth will make him strike till he feels that the right moment has come.

—BERNARD DARWIN, "ALEXANDER (SANDY) HERD" IN
THE DARWIN SKETCHBOOK (WRITINGS FROM 1910 TO 1958)

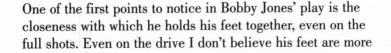

One of the first points to notice in Bobby Jones' play is the closeness with which he holds his feet together, even on the full shots. Even on the drive I don't believe his feet are more than a foot apart, certainly not more than fourteen inches. Frequently on his pitch shots there is less than six inches separating the heels. On the short chip shot his heels are closer still, while in putting they are almost touching.

The matter of bringing the feet closer together than most golfers has two distinct values. In the first place it reduces tension throughout the body. It is more natural to stand with the feet fairly close than it is to spread them out in the broad attitude so many golfers use. In the second place there is a feeling of better and easier balance. There is less tendency to hit with the body, a fault that has driven several million golfers into the borderland of melancholy depression, year after year . . .

There is still another aid to be obtained from this proximity of the feet. It makes the turn of the left hip a simpler, easier matter and this also applies to the transference of the weight where there is less distance to be covered.

—GRANTLAND RICE, "A CLOSE-UP OF BOBBY JONES:
EXPLAINING A FEW OF THE SIMPLER DETAILS THAT MAKE
UP HIS GAME" IN *THE AMERICAN GOLFER* (1927)

The general criticism of the average golfer's posture at address are that his feet are too far apart, his body bent too much, and his arms extended too far. These are the most common faults, and every one of them is unnatural. The natural way to stand is with the feet separated, but not set wide apart, the natural bend of the body is very slight, with weight more back on the heels and never entirely on the toes; and the natural disposition of the arms is to allow them to hang almost straight down from the shoulders . . .

It is very rare that tension is observed in a practice swing, and that is so because the player, not feeling the necessity of being entirely correct, comes closer to assuming natural posture . . .

It will be noted that the better players uniformly address the ball so that the hands of the player are ahead of the ball and the shaft of the club inclines backward to the head, resting behind the ball. This is a very important feature, because the position of the hands assists materially in keeping the club face open. The left hand, being the factor that opens or closes the face, should be placed on the club with the back of the hand upward. This position can only be maintained if the hands are advanced beyond the spot opposite the ball, so that the club will slant backward to its position on the ground.

—BOBBY JONES, *BOBBY JONES ON GOLF* (1966)

The golf swing itself, incorporating the fundamentals, is the focal point of the game. And of that swing, including as it does the grip and stance, the most important feature is the position of the head. So, I think of my head as a hub on a wagon wheel, [and] the position of my arms at the successive stages of the swing as the spokes. That's all. The club head will describe that perfect circle. Sometimes it will go all the way, sometimes it won't, but remove the hub (fall away from the ball, jerk the head toward the side), and you've lost the smooth rhythm that brings results.

—LOUISE SUGGS, "GOLF FOR WOMEN" IN *THE SECRETS OF THE GOLFING GREATS*, EDITED BY TOM SCOTT (1965)

If the ball rebounds to the right of your target, the face (in golf terminology) has been presented "open"; if the ball goes to the left, it has come in "closed." To learn to hit the ball straight consistently, you must be able repeatedly to deliver the face squarely to the ball. You can check to see that you are starting the club face in that position by a simple exercise.

Stand with your feet at shoulder width, your arms hanging in front of you just as you would be if you were about to grip the club. Flex your knees and bend forward at the waist to a position similar to your correct golf posture. Now imagine you are a wheel, a large wagon wheel; your arms are the spokes, and your head is the hub. Start your arms swinging by rotating your trunk and shoulders to the right, letting your arms follow in that direction. Then reverse the direction to the left to unwind the wheel. Gradually increase the turning until your chin is meeting your left shoulder on the backswing and the right shoulder on the follow-through.

—GARY WIREN, *GOLF* (1971)

Anyone who spends a fair amount of time following golf cannot fail to notice what a tremendous number of shots are doomed to failure before the club has gone back an inch, simply because the players are out of distance or standing on the wrong line.

—ENID WILSON, *A GALLERY OF WOMEN GOLFERS* (1961)

Hogan stands decidedly upright with his weight rather forward on the left foot and the right foot drawn a little back. He holds his hands decidedly high, the right hand notably far over, and the right wrist almost arched. The swing is rhythmic and easy and not as long as I expected from the photographs. The club at the top of the swing may in fact go a little past horizontal . . . The impressive part of the swing comes in what books call the hitting area. Then the club head appears to travel with such irresistible speed that it goes right through the ball and far past it before it begins to come up again.

—BERNARD DARWIN, "BEN HOGAN" IN *THE DARWIN SKETCHBOOK* (WRITINGS FROM 1910 TO 1958)

In the relationship between the stance and the arms the left arm is extended and the left elbow is not locked, but straight. Once the grip is assumed with the left hand the left arm automatically becomes part of the shaft.

The shaft of the club should be visualized as a rod from the point of the left shoulder to the club head with one hinge and that being the left wrist. In placing the right hand on the club make sure the right arm is limp and that the right elbow is pointed down.

—BEN HOGAN, *BEN HOGAN'S POWER GOLF* (1948)

Start with a nice little push forward, a waggle or forward press, as we call it, then rebound into your backswing. When you watch a baseball pitcher, you see this. In order to start his movement—to get his motor going— he goes forward first, then back, then forward and *pop!* It's the same way in golf. When you address the ball and just stand there it builds up pressure in the hands, wrists, and arms. This makes it hard to take the club back smoothly and slowly.

—SAM SNEAD, *THE GAME I LOVE* (1997)

Your position at address is very important because it controls both the plane of your swing and your balance. I believe your head should always be behind a line drawn vertically up from the ball. Your knees should be slightly flexed, and you should bend from the waist just far enough to allow your arms to hang in a natural and unrestricted fashion. Set your left arm reasonably straight and firm, so that the club forms a relatively straight line from your left shoulder to the ball. Free your right arm of tension by letting it bend easily at the elbow. This will correctly set your right shoulder lower than your left shoulder, and your right side "under" your left.

—JACK NICKLAUS, *JACK NICKLAUS' LESSON TEE* WITH KEN BOWDEN (1972)

Many beginners fail to get the left hand placed properly and comfortably on the club . . . The golfer should tilt the shaft forward, place his hands so that they ride slightly ahead of the club head, not behind it. The left hand then assumes a strong and natural position. Simultaneously, the face of the club is then poised absolutely square to the line of flight. Some beginners hesitate to adopt this alignment for fear of slicing but, actually, the incorrect position encourages slicing and the correct position does not.

—JOE NOVAK, PROFESSIONAL, BEL AIR COUNTRY CLUB, BEVERLY HILLS, CALIFORNIA, IN *TIPS FROM THE TOP*, EDITED BY HERBERT WARREN WIND (1955)

There is more involved in the correct stance than positions of the feet. When I have taken up what I consider the ideal position for hitting a golf ball, I feel as though I were a tripod with my two feet and the club head as the three points of contact with the ground . . .

When you look at the ideal golf posture from the rear the most noticeable feature is the prominence of the golfer's posterior. The derriere, if I may use the name women's fashion magazines have for it, definitely protrudes. Yet at the same time the line from the waist up to the back of the head is a straight one.

There should be no bend or curve to the back. Both knees should be flexed at all times. What's more, they swing in towards one another. This bending, however, isn't exaggerated. You shouldn't feel that you are knock-kneed, for instance.

—BEN HOGAN, *BEN HOGAN'S POWER GOLF* (1948)

Walter Hagen always said that as long as he kept his legs relaxed he didn't worry. It was his theory—and I agree 100 percent—that with his legs relaxed, the rest of his body would take care of itself. It makes sense. Because when your legs and ankles are supple, then your muscles all can do the work you want them to do. Only then can you pivot correctly and get that sense of rhythm and timing which helps you to go back in one piece and start down from the top with everything working in close harmony.

—SAM SNEAD, *SAM SNEAD'S BASIC GUIDE TO GOOD GOLF* (1961)

Sooner or later golf must become a habit if you want to succeed. As you become proficient, you find yourself doing the same thing the same way time after time. One area in which it is especially important to have a set pattern is in setting up to the ball. I have a three-step pattern that brings me up to the point when I'm ready to start waggling the club. First I size up the shot from behind and to the side of the ball. At the time I check the best line to the target and consider the proposed flight of the ball. Next I place the club head squarely behind the ball so that the club face looks down the target line. Finally I assume my stance.

—ARNOLD PALMER, *THE ARNOLD PALMER METHOD* (1959)

Any woman who can dance can easily learn the footwork of a golf swing. You shift your weight from the left heel to the right heel as you take the club back, then from the right heel to the left as you bring the club forward.

—MARLENE FLOYD, IN *A WOMEN'S GOLF GAME*
BY SHIRLI KASKIE (1982)

Going back, the left foot rolls aggressively onto its inside edge in response to the pull on the legs created by the upper-body turn. Coming down, I push off with an increasing roll onto the inside edge of my right foot as my leg/hip action transfers my weight onto my left side. Through the ball, my leg action, combined with the right-foot thrusting, also causes a rolling of the left foot toward the target. At the end of the follow-through I feel as though I'm carrying 95 percent of my weight on the outside of my left foot.

—JACK NICKLAUS, *JACK NICKLAUS' LESSON TEE*
WITH KEN BOWDEN (1972)

Another chief fault among those who play too infrequently is the habit of raising the left heel too far off the ground on the backswing. I have seen players lift their heel as much as five or six inches and it just has to pull their heads "off the ball" at the top of the backswing. You will rarely see a professional

golfer who lifts his left heel more than an inch and a half or two inches off the ground and from six through the wedge most of them play the shot without the heel leaving the ground at all.
— SAM SNEAD, *SAM SNEAD'S BASIC GUIDE TO GOOD GOLF* (1961)

The stance a golfer employs largely determines the direction in which the shots will fly. There are three stances in golf—square, closed, and open. All things being equal, the square stance will produce a straight shot. The club head will be moving along the line to the target when it strikes the ball. Then the ball will fly with the perfect backspin—no sidespin that would make it fly left or right.

From a closed stance, however, the club head will be moving from inside to outside the target line during impact. This will impart a right-to-left spin that will make the ball hook to the left. The open stance will cause the club head to move to the ball from outside to inside the target line. A left-to-right spin results, causing the ball to slice to the right.
— ARNOLD PALMER, *THE ARNOLD PALMER METHOD* (1959)

Perhaps the most important general aspect of a good putting stance is that you should feel comfortable over the ball. The correct stance is a strong yet relaxed position. All professionals try to develop a putting stance that locks them in place. This helps prevent body movement during the stroke, and yet at the same time keeps the player as loose and free as possible. My knees are slightly bent, but otherwise the legs are straight. The weight should be slightly more on the left foot than on the right. This seems to make it easier to hit the ball solidly.
— BOB ROSBURG, *THE PUTTER BOOK* (1963)

Any putting stoke that swings in an arc suspended from somewhere around your sternum (or some other spot between your shoulders) will have a bottom to its arc, a low point, a place where the sole of the club is closest to the ground. I have found that the best place to position the ball in your stance is approximately two inches . . .

A narrow stance makes it too easy for the golfer to move and rotate the lower body. Furthermore, a narrow stance isn't stable enough to resist being pushed around in the wind . . .

To establish a stable base for your stroke, take a stance width that is at least as wide as your shoulders as measured from the centerline of each shoulder to the center of each shoulder. Even wider stances are okay, but narrower is not.

—DAVE PELZ, *DAVE PELZ'S PUTTING BIBLE* (2000)

The wedge should be gripped lightly—for feel—but firmly in the last three fingers of the left hand so it won't turn upon entering turf or sand . . . I don't move the ball around in my stance. I play all shots off the left heel. The only difference is in the position of the right foot. You move it to the left on shorter shots and back to the right foot on longer shots . . . I feel that the position of the ball in relation to the left foot should be constant for most shots with all clubs.

The stance for the basic sand shot should be more open than on fairway wedge shots, the right foot closer than the left to the intended line of flight. This will automatically produce swing-arc changes designed to put more backspin on the ball. The ball should be positioned on a line extending from slightly behind the left heel. A more open stance shortens the length of the backswing. The open stance also causes the club head to move slightly outside its normal path on the backswing and to slice across the ball at impact . . . There should be very little body action on the sand shot swing . . . The swing is mostly with the hands, arms, and wrists.

—DOUG FORD, *THE WEDGE BOOK* (1963)

Be sure to flex your knees; bend from the waist, which brings the hands and the club closer to the body. Don't grip the club firmly with the right hand. The grip, posture, and body motion are key. Swing the club, don't hit the ball. A good posture follows a good grip, and good posture leads to a good swing. Topping the ball, for example, is a result of bad posture. Keep your head down, [and your] left arm straight, and bend those knees. You're going to hit the ball just because it gets in the way. The practice swing is important. Swing the same way when you hit the ball. We have "crazy" days at our golf course. We make our students wear goggles with tape over them so they can't see the ball. They just focus on adopting the right stance and swinging the club properly.

—PAUL PARKER, HEAD PROFESSIONAL, BUFFALO DUNES
GOLF COURSE, GARDEN CITY, KANSAS (2000)

Practice getting the right relationship of shoulders and chin— your left shoulder should cover the chin in the backswing and the right one cover it in the follow-through. Practice swinging back and through to feel the relationship of chin and shoulders—and do it with your mouth open. This gives an even more definite feeling to chin and shoulder. Remember that this is a woman's problem. Men just don't do it.

—VIVIEN SAUNDERS, *THE GOLF HANDBOOK FOR WOMEN* (2000)

Among the most important elements of the golf stance are:

1. Make sure you have a good grip
2. Look down the target line with hips square
3. Be certain you have good posture
4. Keep the club square to the target
5. Position your body square to the target line

Body type dictates the setup. For example a tall, lanky person might have a shoulder-wide stance, little tilt from the hips, arms riding along his chest. He has lots of arm flexibility to keep the club in front and have a one-piece takeaway. Davis Love is this type of golfer. But you can't teach everyone the same way. For example, a more thick-chested golfer like Craig Stadler must tilt from the waist more to get the club to slide back properly on the takeaway.

—SEAN TAYLOR, PROFESSIONAL, DUKE UNIVERSITY
GOLF CLUB, DURHAM, NORTH CAROLINA (2000)

Another reason my short-iron play has improved is because of my posture. I stand a little taller now, with my chin up. I used to set up too close to the ball and lean over with my head down. Now I'm in a much more athletic position.

—TIGER WOODS, "STAND TALL FOR GOOD POSTURE"
IN *GOLF DIGEST* (2000)

CHAPTER 5

THE SWING

Many professionals have had to manufacture a swing, sometimes going through a major deconstruction and reconstruction with a golf guru such as David Leadbetter. The average golfer might visit a local swing doctor to correct mechanical flaws. Sam Snead, who won more PGA Tour events than any other golfer, is said to be a natural, having imitated the swings of others, beginning with his brother Homer, then refining a grace and tempo all his own. Sam advises that "playing golf is like eating. It's something that has to come naturally."

His advice on swinging the woods is as follows:

It is extremely important, as you start your swing back, that you do not pick up the club by immediately cocking the wrists or you will ruin your rhythm and timing. The arms are almost belt high before the wrists are cocked to generate extra power, preserving balance and creating a return pattern to the spot where on the downswing, the wrists and hands begin to explode their stored-up power into the hit. The left arm meanwhile has been fully extended—throughout the backswing and downswing—without bending the left elbow and with the right elbow kept close to the body.

What Young Tom Morris had was balance and what gave him that was keeping his head steady . . . With the steady head serving as the hub of the axis of the swing there was introduced into golf an essential of uniformity and sound mechanics.

Before the youthful Morris, the foremost players swayed all over Scotland while they were swinging. They lunged at the ball and flogged it. Only by lucky timing, promoted by many hours of play, did a player manage to connect well with the ball.

—HERB GRAFFIS, *ESQUIRE'S WORLD OF GOLF* (1965)

Back at St. Andrews the restraint of the clothing affected the golf swing. Those jackets were tight! In fact, I believe that was the single biggest influence on the early golf swings. You had to sway off the ball and let your left arm bend on the backswing to get full motion. Also, golfers had to let go with the last three fingers of their left hand at the top of the swing. It was the only way they could get the shaft behind their heads.

—GARY MCCORD, *GOLF FOR DUMMIES* (1999)

For the first past (i.e., until the club head reaches the ball) you have a guide implied in the above-noted fact that the downward stroke is a reproduction of the upward. Tutor yourself by letting your arms gradually go to their full length as you raise the club, and of themselves they will come to repeat the motion. Conversely, as it descends. For accomplishing the latter part of the stroke, after the ball is struck, successfully, two things are requisite—that your grip on the club should be light with the right hand, and that your right shoulder should work free and loose.

—HORACE HUTCHINSON, *HINTS ON THE GAME OF GOLF* (1886)

With a fairly steady axis of the swing having been established the next advance in golf's technology naturally would come the spoke of the swing. This progress wasn't made quickly. For years the best of the golfers wheeled around onto the ball with a flat swing. Sargent thought that the hickory shaft and the design of wood and iron heads to get the hard molded gutta percha ball up off the thinly grassed fairways and out of tangled rough and sand of Scotch links, probably favored retention of a swing that was primarily a matter of body turn and comparatively minor hand action.

Then came along Harry Vardon to turn attention to the manner of coupling player and club and manipulating the club so its face could be controlled with reasonable nearness to precision, thus the club head could be accelerated by the wrists smoothly into required speed as the ball was hit.

—HERB GRAFFIS ON HARRY VARDON, WHO WON THREE BRITISH OPENS WITH THE "GUTTY" AND THREE WITH THE WOUND AND MOLDED RUBBER-COVER BALL, IN *ESQUIRE'S WORLD OF GOLF* (1965)

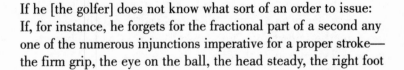

The head must necessarily be steady, for it is most important that you should keep your eye fixedly on the ball from the moment that the club head is lifted from the ground until the ball is actually struck. "Keep your eye on the ball" should be your companion text to "slow back."

—HORACE HUTCHINSON, *HINTS ON THE GAME OF GOLF* (1886)

If he [the golfer] does not know what sort of an order to issue: If, for instance, he forgets for the fractional part of a second any one of the numerous injunctions imperative for a proper stroke— the firm grip, the eye on the ball, the head steady, the right foot fixed, the rhythmic backswing, the twirl of the wrists, the accelerated velocity, the hit at impact, the glorious follow-through, to say nothing of the preliminary stance, waggle, judging of distance, and correct angle of feet, elbows, body, and what-not, well all I can say is that woe betides him.

—ARNOLD HAULTAIN, *THE MYSTERY OF GOLF* (1908)

Usually when a player makes a really bad stroke you see him trying the swing over again—without the ball—wondering what went wrong. It would pay him much better to do the good strokes over again in the same way every time he makes them, so as to impress the method of execution firmly in his mind.

—HARRY VARDON, *THE COMPLETE GOLFER* (1905)

Now the secret of all strokes at golf, with the exception of certain refined strokes played for the most part with iron, is to make the club travel as long as possible in the direction in which you wish the ball to go, consistently with the application of sufficient force—that is, with sufficient speed of impact . . .

The proper line of motion can only be given to the club head by grasping lightly with the right hand, keeping the right shoulder down and its muscles loose . . .

All preliminary adjustments thus completed, we come to the magnum opus—the swing proper. Now the upward part of the swing is only important for the bearing upon the downward. But in this respect its importance is very great; and I would ask you to accept this as an axiom—"that the head of the club should describe the same figure in its upward journey as you hope to make it describe in its descent."

—HORACE HUTCHINSON, *HINTS ON THE GAME OF GOLF* (1886)

Vardon certainly made no fetish of the stiff arm. Another thing is the uniform beauty of the follow-through. Time after time he would come right through, drawn to his full height, the club right down over his left shoulder, the hands well up, the left elbow tolerably high. It was the ideal copybook follow-through and he did it every time with an almost monotonous perfection.
—BERNARD DARWIN, "VARDON'S METHOD" IN *THE DARWIN SKETCHBOOK* (WRITINGS FROM 1910 TO 1958)

Nobody ever swung a golf club too slowly.
—BOBBY JONES, *BOBBY JONES ON GOLF* (1966)

First of all, he was a conspicuous example of the doctrine of "hands leading." In his day the books used to tell us that the head of the club should go back first and the wrist begin at once to turn away . . . In Vardon's case, however, it was clear that he did none of these things; one could actually see the hands leading and the club head going back for some distance before he slung it to the top of the swing. Neither does any photograph convey the small but still perceptible touch of lift in the upswing nor the little touch of sway . . .

His was essentially an upright swing in the days when orthodox swings were flat and was the more noticeable accordingly. He took the club up very straight, "too straight," as any self-respecting caddie would have said instructing his master. Then by way of natural compensation he flung the club head well out behind him and brought it down on the ball with a big sweep. It was a beautifully free movement of one having a natural gift for opening his shoulders and hitting clean. And of course, like the movements of really great golfers, it was instinct with that mysterious thing called rhythm. No golfer in the world, not even Bobby himself, was more perfectly rhythmic than Harry Vardon.

—BERNARD DARWIN, "VARDON'S METHOD" IN
THE DARWIN SKETCHBOOK (WRITINGS FROM 1910 TO 1958)

Your club is coming to the horizontal across the right shoulder, a few inches out from the nape of the neck, arrived there by the line it must take in the downswing. There is no going up one way and coming down another. Be careful not to pull the hands in toward the body in coming down. Throw the club head out from you at the start of the descent. The effect of this is to bring the club well behind the ball—and not down on it—for the blow. There must be an element of sweep in the hit, or an element of hit in the sweep.

But unless the club comes at the ball almost on a plane for two or three feet, the result will be a high, short shot at best. The reason for this is easily seen. Without it there can be no follow-through.

—SANDY HERD, "THE THREE TYPES OF PUPIL: WHICH
ARE YOU?" IN *THE AMERICAN GOLFER* MAGAZINE (1923)

Because you hole a bogey, or even sometimes in one stroke less, do not always take it for granted that you have therefore played perfect golf. Some bogeys are very easy, and some shots are very flukey. A man may miss his drive, run a bunker and hole out with his mashie, beating bogey by a stroke. But he would be well advised not to say anything about it afterwards, lest he should be asked for details. Not the smallest credit attaches to him for his remarkable performance.

—HARRY VARDON, "SOME GENERAL HINTS" IN *THE COMPLETE GOLFER:
SECRETS OF THE GOLFING GREATS*, EDITED BY TOM SCOTT (1961)

There are two sides to golf—the mechanical and the mental.
And it's a mighty simple and a sure recipe for improvement if
you'll let it sink into your system. The mechanical side is the
swing—when you have learned the correct swing that part of
your game should be behind you. It is a tool you have acquired
and its use is hitting the ball. And the mental side of golf is not
intense, wrinkle-browed concentration—it's simply stepping up
to the ball with the determination to hit it where you want it to
go, or "hit through it," whichever expression you prefer—with
no other thought in your mind—none whatever.

—EDDIE LOOS, "HIT THE BALL" IN
THE AMERICAN GOLFER MAGAZINE (1922)

Golf is so simple it is difficult. That may be a strange state-
ment, but I believe a true one. When Mr. Ernest Jones tied a
jackknife to a corner of a large handkerchief and proved to
me what swinging actually meant and what a real swing felt
like, I proceeded to forget a multitude of so-called fundamentals and worked solely on one thing—learning to swing the
club head with my hands and letting the rest of my anatomy
follow the swing.

From that day on, not only did my golf improve to the extent
that I was able to win the national championship, but I learned
that the game could be a joy and a pleasure, instead of a mild
form of torture.

—VIRGINIA VAN WIE, "SWINGING THE CLUBHEAD"
IN *THE AMERICAN GOLFER* MAGAZINE (1934)

Never throw the club head. Swing it all the way through. Above
all do not make a "hit" of it. The deliberate, premeditated flick

or throw of the club—either from the top of the swing, waist high as some advocate, or just when coming on the ball—is wrong. It results in mediocre golf, not the finished play of the expert. This holds equally good for the iron shots as for shots with the wood. Aside from putting, there is no purely wrist shot in the whole realm of golf.

—HARRY VARDON TO OWEN BROWN, "A LESSON FROM HARRY VARDON" IN *THE AMERICAN GOLFER* MAGAZINE (1930)

Keeping the left arm straight automatically prevents over-swinging . . . especially with irons, and most especially with lofted irons. With the straight left arm, the player can hardly get the club back too far for a full shot, unless he lifts his hands higher than his head, which he is not likely to do. The straight left arm promotes correct wrist-work if not positively, at least negatively. Maybe it would be better to say it permits or favors correct wrist-work, which is next to impossible and certainly useless with the choppy stoke resulting from the bent left arm.

—STEWART MAIDEN TO O. B. KEELER, "THE MOST COMMON FAULTS" IN *THE AMERICAN GOLFER* MAGAZINE (1922)

To describe her manner of playing is almost impossible. She stands quite close to the ball, she places the club once behind, takes one look toward the objective and strikes. Her swing is not long—surprisingly short, indeed, when one considers the power she develops—but it is rhythmic in the last degree. She makes ample use of her wrists, and her left arm within the hitting area is firm and active. This I think distinguishes her swing from that of any other woman golfer, and it is the one thing that makes her the player she is.

—ROBERT T. JONES JR., "THE GREATEST OF GOLFERS: A TRIBUTE TO THE RARE SKILL OF MISS JOYCE WETHERED" IN *THE AMERICAN GOLFER* MAGAZINE (1930)

Hit means tension—tightening of the muscles. The word *swing* means just the opposite . . . In this swinging motion, the weight moves more easily from left to right, than from right to left, just as the hands and arms and club head travel. I think the basis of control after the swing starts is hitting against the left leg. So I make sure that my left heel is back and that my left side is in place. If the left leg isn't ready to catch and hold the swing at the moment of impact, it is impossible to have any power left or to have any control . . . I just swing against the left side, this also helps to keep my head in place and prevent my looking up.

—MACDONALD SMITH, "SWING, DON'T HIT" IN *THE AMERICAN GOLFER* MAGAZINE (1930)

Supreme ability to wait for the club head on the tee shot, never hurrying the stroke, and never forcing the body in to gain extra distance. A closed stance with the right foot well behind the left to give free play to the push of the body and the roll of the hips as the ball is met. Hands well over the shaft, the ball of the left hand controlling the grip and working with the fingers of that hand to keep the club in full control at all times. This particularly with the iron clubs.

—WALTER R. MCCALLUM, "HOW ARMOUR DOES IT: THE SECRETS OF HIS SUPERB SKILL AND HOW HE ACQUIRED THEM" IN *THE AMERICAN GOLFER* MAGAZINE (1927)

Before starting any discussion of the golf swing, I should like first to say that my own impression is that most golfers go quite the wrong way about learning the game. This refers to being always on the alert to find out what is wrong instead of getting to know what is right.

—ERNEST JONES, "SWING THE CLUBHEAD: A PLEA
FOR SIMPLICITY IN ANALYZING THE GOLF SWING"
IN *THE AMERICAN GOLFER* MAGAZINE (1927)

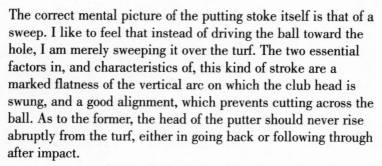

The correct mental picture of the putting stoke itself is that of a sweep. I like to feel that instead of driving the ball toward the hole, I am merely sweeping it over the turf. The two essential factors in, and characteristics of, this kind of stroke are a marked flatness of the vertical arc on which the club head is swung, and a good alignment, which prevents cutting across the ball. As to the former, the head of the putter should never rise abruptly from the turf, either in going back or following through after impact.

—ROBERT T. JONES JR., "THE ART OF GOOD PUTTING"
IN *THE AMERICAN GOLFER* MAGAZINE (1933)

The arc described by the head of a golf club is governed by the length of the shaft and the extent of the player's left arm. The club head travels on an oblique plane, in parallel with the line of play. Any irregularity in the plane, or deviation from the line interferes with the rhythm of the swing and spoils the accuracy of the stroke . . .

"How do I hit it?" The answer being, she does not hit the ball, the function is performed by the club head. The less the player knows and thinks about what is happening during the swing, the better are her chances of permitting the operative end of the club to fulfill its task. In order to let the club head do the work, it must be allowed to lead. When it is swung properly the player is not conscious of what is happening to her hands, arms, shoulders, hips, knees, or feet, their movements being blended into the rhythm of the stroke. The perfectly timed swing is effortless, but it defies dissection. Taken apart it becomes an assortment of ill-matched components.

—ENID WILSON, "FUNCTION OF THE CLUB—SWINGS AND STYLES" IN *SECRETS OF THE GOLFING GREATS*, EDITED BY TOM SCOTT (1965)

A shank—the shot where the ball goes off the joint of the shaft and the club head at any angle except the intended one—is the most terrifying one in golf. It strikes without warning, often in the middle of a good round. From the moment a golfer shanks, he becomes a different man. From the easy, happy-go-lucky golfer of a moment before, he becomes a shaking jelly of a man unable to explain why he finds it difficult to hit the ball.

—DAI REES, "COMMON FAULTS" IN *SECRETS OF THE GOLFING GREATS*, EDITED BY TOM SCOTT (1965)

Sometime in the 1940s, though, American golfers began to overemphasize and complicate swing mechanics. They began to forget the wisdom that Stewart Maiden passed along to Bobby Jones and that Walter Hagen and Sam Snead discovered for themselves. This was not, of course, true everywhere. Golf is a sport of individuals and everyone had his own approach to the game. Teachers like Harvey Penick never stopped imparting sound principles about the mental side of golf. But they became a minority.

—BOB ROTELLA, *GOLF IS NOT A GAME OF PERFECT* (1997)

When the pros get up to the top and then halfway down, at hip high, the shaft is pointing into the ball again halfway down. If you do that you can just relax and hit the ball long. One good thing to practice: Take it back halfway; point the shaft at the ball; and release and point it back at the ball, and hit maybe fifty or one hundred balls a day doing that. Because you can check it out yourself.

—JOHNNY MILLER (1998)

A woman's center of gravity is lower than a man's. A woman's weight is centered on her hips, a man's on his shoulders. His hips can move about during the swing without affecting the groove. In order to free her shoulders it is necessary for a woman to get the weight on her right foot. When she does this she tilts the pelvic area and permits the big muscles of the back to have freer action. The transference should be without any knee or hip turn, merely the transference of weight, shifted as the club begins to go back.

—MRS. STUART HANLEY, IN *A GALLERY OF WOMEN GOLFERS* BY ENID WILSON (1961)

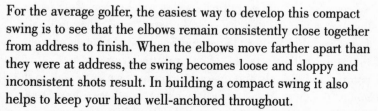

For the average golfer, the easiest way to develop this compact swing is to see that the elbows remain consistently close together from address to finish. When the elbows move farther apart than they were at address, the swing becomes loose and sloppy and inconsistent shots result. In building a compact swing it also helps to keep your head well-anchored throughout.

—ARNOLD PALMER, *THE ARNOLD PALMER METHOD* (1959)

Many golfers have entirely the wrong notion of what the head is supposed to do. They have been warned: "Keep Your Head Down." "Keep Your Eye on the Ball." "Don't Move Your Head." This leads them to stay in a fixed position which is completely unnatural. It is humanly impossible to turn your shoulders into the desired position and still keep your face pointed straight down at the ground. In doing this, you would disastrously restrict the backswing. However, your eyes should still be on the ball.

—LOUISE SUGGS, *PAR GOLF FOR WOMEN* (1953)

As a young player, I would watch other swings very carefully and try parts of swings. I liked to see if they fit mine. Usually, I ended up discarding the new piece, but it was fun to see what I could invent in my "laboratory." Who knows how it all fit together at the end?

The first person I actually played with was my brother, Homer, who was twelve years older than me. We laid out a four-hole course, sank some tomato cans for cups, and hit around rocks with crooked sticks for hours. Homer had a long flowing swing, and he could generate power! I would watch him swing, and I guess you could say I copied his swing.

—SAM SNEAD, *THE GAME I LOVE* (1997)

Actually there is a slight variation in swing from club to club, but you should not make a conscious effort to swing one club differently than another. The natural variation is caused by the different positions in which you must stand to hit the ball for the great variety of lies encountered on any course, and the range of shaft lengths and club head angles.

For instance, in using a driver you stand the farthest from the ball because the club shaft is longer, the club head at a flatter angle to the shaft, and the ball is teed up . . . I am completely unaware of making any attempt to swing one club differently than another.

—BYRON NELSON, *BYRON NELSON'S WINNING GOLF* (1946)

The swing:

1. Address: At address, you should be standing tall and relaxed, with arms and club hanging in a Y shape.
2. Takeaway: Make sure the toe of your club is pointing upward at takeaway.
3. Top of the backswing: Your back should be facing the target and the club supported on your left thumb.
4. Impact: Good impact is all about brushing the grass and ball at exactly the right spot.
5. Follow-through: The toe of the club should be pointing upward, matching the takeaway.
6. Finish: Your body should be facing the target, with the club shaft settled neatly on your left shoulder.

—VIVIEN SAUNDERS, *THE GOLF HANDBOOK FOR WOMEN* (2000)

Too many golfers permit the left arm to collapse as they start the downswing. At this point they allow the right hand, arm, and side to take charge of making the shot. When the right hand takes charge, the club moves outside the correct line or groove and is pulled back across the line of flight in contacting the ball. This is why so many weekend golfers are cursed with a slice . . .

Another factor which causes a slice . . . is the slight opening of the fingers of the left hand at the top of the backswing. As the downswing is started, the hand is tightened unconsciously. This causes the club head to loop as you start your downswing and throws it across the line of flight to cause a slice. So keep those left fingers firm at the top of the backswing—feeling the firmness with the key little finger—and save yourself a lot of headaches.

—SAM SNEAD, *SAM SNEAD'S GUIDE TO BASIC GOLF* (1961)

In fact there is no such thing as leverage in golf at all. It is the speed that is required: Leverage and speed don't go together. Momentum and speed, yes: but not leverage. In a full swing you move the club head with the hands as far as your wrists will allow you to go, both backward and forward, of course letting the arms, shoulders, and body give, so as to get the right balance. In a shoulder swing the wrists give according to how far the club is moved, so that in a short putt they would hardly give at all. For comparison take the action of a man driving a pile with a sledgehammer, and a jeweler using his hammer on a watch; it all depends on the amount of power applied.

—ERNEST JONES, "SWING THE CLUBHEAD: A PLEA
FOR SIMPLICITY IN ANALYZING THE GOLF SWING"
IN *THE AMERICAN GOLFER* MAGAZINE (1927)

My distance comes from leverage. My leverage comes from a big body turn on the backswing. Most high-handicap golfers lack distance because, in place of a turn, they lift the club with their hands and arms. That's a lazy way to make a backswing and it results in an unacceptable shot. Other high-handicappers lack distance because, although they turn some parts of their body, they do so in a direction or in a sequence that fails to produce torsion, the necessary wind-up or coiling. They build no snap into the spring at the top . . .

—JACK NICKLAUS, *JACK NICKLAUS' LESSON TEE*
WITH KEN BOWDEN (1972)

No golf swing can be built without rhythm. Rhythm to me is like a child's play swing. Once it is swung back in motion it will reach its own stopping point at the top and start down again of its own accord and momentum. No conscious effort should ever be made to interrupt, accelerate, or slow down the natural motion and momentum of a golf swing, for good rhythm therein is a slow and gradual buildup of both power and speed from the time the club head addresses the ball until it contacts it and completes the swing with the power of its own momentum . . .

Rhythm is an entity unto itself. Like death and taxes, don't question it; just accept it. You must.

—MICKEY WRIGHT, *PLAY GOLF THE WRIGHT WAY* (1962)

Notice I didn't say swing hard . . . Try to think of your golf swing as an efficient machine. Each part is dependent on the other parts; if one part is functioning incorrectly the others will be affected. But working together they deliver the same effective result time after time. This is your objective. Build the most efficient machine you can.

—JULIUS BOROS, *SWING EASY, HIT HARD* (1965)

The beginning of the backswing almost always "programs" the remainder of the swing. This being the case, here are some factors that play a big part in my takeaway:

1. I swing the club straight back from the ball, without breaking my wrists, for as long as the turning of my shoulders and hips will allow, so that I may receive the broadest possible swing arc.
2. I try to keep the club face square to the target line as long as possible, never turning my hands and wrists under to hold the club face artificially on that line.
3. I try to keep my left arm and club in a straight line until the sheer momentum of the swinging club head causes my wrists to cock naturally.

Unfortunately, many golfers develop a full swing in the worst possible way by letting the club go loose in their hands at the top. This is usually the result of "lazy" body action, lifting the club with the hands and arms instead of turning the shoulders on the backswing. Another cause is too fast a backswing— yanking the club back so fast the fingers can't control it at the top . . .

—JACK NICKLAUS, *JACK NICKLAUS' LESSON TEE*
WITH KEN BOWDEN (1972)

There are two approaches to striking a golf ball—swinging and hitting . . . To develop consistency in a hard-hitting swing like Arnold Palmer's takes years of practice and the hitting of thousands of practice balls. In addition, it requires a great deal of playing and practice to maintain the timing for successful repetition.

—GARY WIREN, *GOLF* (1971)

Club head speed is the result of club, arms, shoulders, hips, legs—everything working together. Go ahead and swing with all of your physical motion when you're learning how to swing a golf club. It can become a natural thing. So what if your shots spray all over at first. You will straighten them out once you have the idea, so swing the club hard.

—HOLLIS STACY, *A WOMAN'S GOLF GAME* (1982)

He [Sam Snead] made me realize how important rhythm is, how important the speed of the golf swing is. Sam was the master of that. I've known Sam now for thirty-one years and even today with all his ailments and being up in age, he still has a fantastic rhythm to his swing.

—RAYMOND FLOYD, IN *GOLF DIGEST* (1994)

Much of the inconsistency of putting is the result of the complexity of the way golfers swing their putters . . . The building blocks of the game are aim, path, touch, rhythm, ritual, feel, face angle, stability, attitude, routine, putter fitting, power source, impact pattern, flow-lines, green-reading . . . The good news is that most golfers (you included) are usually pretty good at most of these putting-skill blocks. The bad news is that few golfers have all fifteen of them formed and polished well enough to make putting a strength of their game.

—DAVE PELZ, *DAVE PELZ'S PUTTING BIBLE* (2000)

If you want to add more zip to your woods and long irons, try emulating a discus thrower when you swing. The same coil-and-release motion that characterizes the discus throw also generates power in a golf swing . . .

The unwinding of the upper body provides speed and power as the player shifts toward the target. In fact the golfer should try to mimic the right-hand motion of the discus thrower in the follow-through, swinging upward through impact with the palm rotating toward the ground. This up-and-around motion, with the right forearm rotating over the left encourages a full release through the shot and a powerful draw.

—JERRY MOULDS, DIRECTOR OF INSTRUCTION AT PUMPKIN RIDGE, NORTH PLAINS, OREGON, IN *GOLF MAGAZINE* (2000)

Many golfers lose much of the power they've created on the way back by unlocking their wrists too early on the way down. To maximize your club-head speed, delay the uncocking of the wrists until just before impact. Learn to increase your club-head lag with this simple drill: Hold the fingers of your right hand in a "cocked" position as you slowly swing your arms down. As you approach the impact position, release the fingers to snap the right hand forward. That's the feeling you want as you whip the club through the ball.

—DAVID LEADBETTER, "HIT IT FARTHER, STRAIGHTER, CLOSER" IN *GOLF DIGEST* (2000)

You need to get more out of your swing. Sometimes you get so afraid of hitting bad shots, we don't let ourselves hit good ones.

—BUTCH HARMON, IN *SPORTS ILLUSTRATED* (2000)

Here are some simple thoughts to help you get some needed yardage: Turn your shoulders on the backswing. The more you turn your shoulders on the backswing, the better chance you have to hit the ball longer. So stretch that torso on the backswing, and try to put your left shoulder over the right foot at the top of your swing . . . Grip the club loosely—remember, you should grip it with the pressure of holding a spotted owl's egg . . . Turning your hips to the left on the downswing and extending your right arm on the through-swing are trademarks of the longer hitters.

—GARY McCORD, *GOLF FOR DUMMIES* (1999)

When it comes to the swing, the most important factor is the turn. Get your club back into position to swing down the target line. Too many players use their upper body only, go outside the line, then go left or right of the ideal swing path. Make sure your weight is on your right side initially, then shift left. Too many players go outside in, without a proper turn, and then slice the ball.

—TOM SMACK, DIRECTOR OF GOLF AND HEAD PROFESSIONAL, THE SAGAMORE GOLF CLUB, BOLTON LANDING, NEW YORK (2000)

Realize there is no one perfect swing. Swings are like personalities. Develop a consistent swing and keep it simple as possible. Find a model or ideal swing suited to your body type and style. If you are short and heavy, Craig Stadler might be a better model than Tiger Woods. Learn by watching and visualize a successful swing. Related to your game and swing, be realistic about what might be a successful playing strategy for you. For example, you might be better able to hit a successful five-iron shot on the fairway rather than topping a three-wood.

—RICK POHLE, HEAD PROFESSIONAL, TACONIC GOLF CLUB, WILLIAMSTOWN, MASSACHUSETTS (2000)

This may sound strange, but playing from a stance that works against your club face problem is a very reliable way to control shot shape . . . If you match your feet to your face, you'll get rid of those crooked shots . . .

To fix a slice . . . take your normal stance then flare your left foot out about 45 degrees toward the target. This position restricts hip rotation away from the target going back, thereby creating a tighter coil between the upper body and the lower body and, in effect, presetting rapid hip rotation toward the target on the forward swing. And faster torso rotation means faster closing rotation of the club face and therefore straighter shots.

—TOM STICKNEY II WITH PETER MORRICE, SENIOR GOLFER (2000)

CHAPTER 6

OFF THE TEE: THE DRIVE

The noted golf instructor Jim Flick cautions that the driver often causes problems off the tee because it theoretically has no distance limitations. This sometimes can lead to an out-of-control power swing that wreaks havoc on distance and accuracy. Flick recommends high- to mid-handicappers use a three-wood off the tee rather than a driver.

Glenna Collett, then a girl of fourteen in her native Rhode Island, noted in her biography, *Ladies in the Rough*, the seductiveness of the driver:

> Standing on the broad veranda [at the Matacomet Golf Club], perched high on a Rhode Island hill, I watched Dad send a long, raking tee shot through the air. It dropped far down the fairway.
>
> Tremendously impressed, I hurried out on the course and asked for permission to play along with him. With beginner's luck my first shot off the tee went straight down the fairway. The length and accuracy of my initial drive stirred the enthusiasm of my father and several spectators.

Collett later won six U.S. Women's Amateurs, still a record.

Now, wherein lies the difficulty of hitting that unresisting piece of gutta-percha? Everyone knows that there are about twenty-two things to attend to in making a drive, but it may suffice to mention three or four. For instance, grasp, balance, keeping your eye on the ball, and letting your arms follow the ball.

—LORD WELLWOOD, "GENERAL REMARKS ON THE GAME" IN *THE BADMINTON LIBRARY: GOLF* (1890)

Not only is the stroke in golf an extremely difficult one, it is also an extremely complicated one, more especially the drive, in which its principles are accentuated. It is in fact a subtle combination of a swing and a hit; the "hit" portion being deftly incorporated into the "swing" portion. Just as the head of the club reaches the ball, yet without disturbing the regular rhythm of the motion.

—ARNOLD HAULTAIN, *THE MYSTERY OF GOLF* (1908)

In addressing the ball when driving, Willie's position differed from most golfers, his right foot being a little in front, instead of his left. He had as pretty a swing as one could wish to see. It was not what you would call a long swing, but a beautiful round swing. The club did not descend away down the back almost to the ground, as is the case with many possessing a very long swing, but described as it were, a circle round the head. So clean did he hit the ball, and with such force, that on many occasions when I have stood close behind him, the meeting of the club and the ball sounded more like the report of a pistol than anything else.

—A. H. DOLEMAN DESCRIBING THE SWING OF WILLIE PARK SR., *THE PARKS OF MUSSELBURGH* (1991)

In the swing of a first-rate slashing driver there are but two portions of the body which are comparatively steady—his head, and the toes and the balls of his feet.

- The head must be steady.
- You should keep your eye fixedly on the ball from the moment that the club head is lifted from the ground until the ball is actually struck.
- Be content to swing with the upper part of the body only— and swing quietly with that.
- The club head will so describe that arc not of a circle but an ellipse.
- The arms must in fact be, as it were, thrown away from the body at the end of the stroke.

—HORACE HUTCHINSON, *HINTS ON GOLF* (1886)

Above everything, the golfing drive is a swing, and not a hit. These are very short and simple words and contain a truth universally admitted—universally, almost forgotten . . . It may be almost termed a sweep: The ball is to be met by the club head at a certain point in the swing, and swept away; it is not to be hit at . . . The former [the hit] is delivered with a jerk and with tightened muscles, the latter is a motion whose speed is gained by the gradual not jerky acceleration with muscles flexible . . .

—HORACE HUTCHINSON, "ELEMENTARY INSTRUCTION: DRIVING"
IN *THE BADMINTON LIBRARY: GOLF* (1890)

He was the most accurate of all the wooden club players of the day and yet a first sight of him would hardly have conveyed it. Imagine a short man (he is five feet six inches in height) with a long club placing his feet with meticulous care in regard to the line and then rather sitting down to the ball. The waggle is careful and restrained; then suddenly all is changed; he seems almost to jump on to his toes in the upswing and fairly to fling himself at the ball . . .

—BERNARD DARWIN, "HAROLD HILTON" IN *THE DARWIN SKETCHBOOK* (WRITINGS FROM 1910 TO 1958)

I can remember very well the first time I saw him play. It was in the late summer of 1896, and he had won his first [British Open] Championship in the spring. I went over to Ganton, where he was then professional, for a day's golf and there by good luck was the great man driving off. He hit just the sort of drive that he always did—dead straight and rather high, the ball seeming to float with a particularly lazy flight through the air. The shot was obviously a perfect one and yet I was not quite so impressed as I expected to be. The style was so different from what I had been taught to admire; the club seemed to be taken up in so outrageously upright a manner, with something of a lift.

—BERNARD DARWIN, "VARDON'S METHOD"
IN *THE DARWIN SKETCHBOOK*
(WRITINGS FROM 1910 TO 1958)

Above everything, it is necessary to be on one's guard against letting the weight of the body fall forward onto the left leg at the top of the backswing. In my view, it is absurd to expect a good drive from such an attitude.

The average player tees the ball too low for the drive. The fine player tees the ball high, usually with about half of the ball being above the top of the driver when it is soled behind the ball . . . Before we get away from the subject of learning

how to tee a ball, always tee your ball on the short holes . . .
One thing I always advise is to use a club with a shaft a little
bit whippier than you might want it to be. The big idea is to
have the club working for you, instead of against you.

—TOMMY ARMOUR, *HOW TO PLAY YOUR*
BEST GOLF ALL THE TIME (1953)

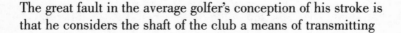

Let the right shoulder go back an inch or two while the head is
kept fairly still; let the right leg share with the left leg the weight
of the body in about the proportion of three-fifths to two-fifths; it
will then be felt that you can hit the ball with all your might, and
in doing so bring the right shoulder smoothly through after the
ball has been struck. The speed of the club head must be considerably faster by taking up this position than if more of the
weight were thrown on the left leg than the right . . .

Sometimes it is said of me that I belong to the class of golfers
who rely on swaying—and the timing of it—for length. I do not
sway so much as may be thought. In fact, I should say that the
camera would support my contention that all the swaying I do
is after the ball has been dispatched. Then I often feel myself,
not only throwing the right shoulder through and head with it,
but actually getting off my right foot and walking after the ball.
That may be called swaying, but it is the kind of swaying a
boxer uses in delivering a blow.

—TED RAY, "GETTING DISTANCE ON THE DRIVE:
THE ESSENTIALS OF LONG HITTING FROM THE TEE"
IN *THE AMERICAN GOLFER* MAGAZINE (1924)

The great fault in the average golfer's conception of his stroke is
that he considers the shaft of the club a means of transmitting

actual physical force to the ball, whereas in reality it is merely the means of imparting velocity to the club head. We would all do better could we only realize that the length of a drive depends not upon the brute force applied but the speed of the club head. It is a matter of velocity rather than physical effort of the kind that bends crowbars and lifts heavy weights.

I like to think of a golf club as a weight attached to my hands by an imponderable medium, to which a string is a close approximation; and I like to feel that I am throwing it at the ball with much the same motion I should use in cracking a whip.

—BOBBY JONES, *BOBBY JONES ON GOLF* (1966)

On my normal driver swing, I would always drop my right foot back a little, giving me more room to turn and promoting an aggressive inside attack. With this alignment I could play a nice draw and feel a nice easy turn.

If I had to play a hook or a real "coat hanger," as we called it, I would drop my right heel back even more and give the shot more right-to-left spin.

To play a fade, I just opened up by dropping my left foot back a little to cut across the ball a bit.

I didn't really like the idea of changing the swing as such, because that was already grooved or automatic.

—SAM SNEAD, *THE GAME I LOVE* (1997)

My feet are as far apart as the width of my shoulders. My toes are out, weight back through the feet, knees flexed and bent in toward the other. The right arm is relaxed and lower than the left. The left elbow is pointing toward the left hip and the right elbow toward the right hip. This shot calls for a full application of power, but note the absence of any appearance of strain.

—BEN HOGAN, *BEN HOGAN'S POWER GOLF* (1948)

When you are addressing the ball, your arms should be comfortably fixed, not extended rigidly . . . One method which I personally find helpful is to address the ball slightly off the toe of the club. During the swing the arms are bound to do some stretching, for they extend themselves naturally. This stretching brings the center of the club head squarely into the ball. It is not a conscious effort to "reach for the ball." You simply arrive at the ball, your arms fully extended as they should be, but muscularly alive.

—MIKE TURNESA, "THE RELAXED ADDRESS"
IN *TIPS FROM THE TOP*, EDITED BY
HERBERT WARREN WIND (1955)

Impact with woods is different from impact with irons. Because you want the ball to fly and roll as far as possible, you must eliminate the backspin. To do this you must hit through the ball but not down on it. Thus the ball is contacted on the upswing or as the ball runs parallel to the ground, giving us a forward or rolling spin.

—JULIUS BOROS, *SWING EASY, HIT HARD* (1965)

The ball flies high and may tend to fade from left to right. [Use this shot] with the wind behind the shot, with especially hard fairways, or with especially lush fairways, to clear fairway hazards or cut a dogleg corner.

Tee the ball higher, so that two-thirds of it appears over the top of the club head. Position [the] ball off [the] left toe, your hands and head behind the ball. [The] stance is square. Use a full backswing and swing on to a high finish . . .

[To fade a tee shot], first of all, I place the club head behind the ball so that it is facing on a line to the left of the fairway position I'm after. Now—and this is very important—I draw a mental line along the path on which I want to start the ball flying. Using this line as a basis, I assume an open stance, my left foot withdrawn a couple of inches more than the right from this line. A line drawn along my toes would point to the left of my imaginary line.

—BILLY CASPER, *GOLF SHOTMAKING WITH BILLY CASPER* (1966)

Plan the line and length of your target carefully. Ideally choose a target not only on the line you want to hit but roughly the length you want . . . Always aim away from trouble. If there is a bunker at driving distance, don't just aim five yards away from it. Be prepared to aim 20 yards away and allow yourself a greater margin of error. When playing a long hole, or when an opponent drives farther than you do, never try to hit the ball too hard. Concentrate on good timing and hit the ball your normal distance. If you press for length, your direction tends to deteriorate.

—VIVIEN SAUNDERS, *THE GOLF HANDBOOK FOR WOMEN* (2000)

Bring your club back with your shoulders. As you begin your backswing, keep your head still. Sweep your club along the ground about eighteen inches as you gradually turn your upper body and shoulders to bring your arms up to the top of your backswing.

Keep your left arm straight but not rigid. It should never be so rigid as to restrict your shoulder turn. As your shoulders turn, shift your weight to your right side. At the top of your backswing, your left shoulder should be under your chin.

I drive everything to my left side through the target on my downswing. My arms are going to the target. My head comes up naturally to allow me to follow through . . .

A lot of women get into trouble right away with the driver because they try to hit it too hard. Golf is not a power game for a woman. It's a game of accuracy. Concentrate on accuracy. It is also important to stay smooth. Use your normal swing with your driver. Let your club do the work.

—BETH DANIEL, IN *A WOMAN'S GOLF GAME* BY SHIRLI KASKIE (1982)

The swing with the driver should be rounded, making a powerful horizontal attack onto the back of the ball. Remember that the plane of the swing should follow the angle of the club shaft at address. Have the courage to turn away from the ball in the backswing. Make sure that you really do turn your back to the target, rather than just lifting the arms and the club. You want to make a horizontal attack. Think of the contact with the driver as like striking a nail into the back of the ball. The hammer [club head] should move in a shallow curve both back and through. Don't pick the club up as though bending your nail. Follow through for power . . . keep the right shoulder comfortably down at address, the ball just two to three inches ahead of center in the stance and learn the feeling of a low takeaway and low attack.

—VIVIEN SAUNDERS, *THE GOLF HANDBOOK FOR WOMEN* (2000)

Many weekend golfers don't even wait for a bad shot to stop trusting their swing. They step onto the first tee thinking of a dozen mechanical concepts they've heard from friends, read about in magazines, or seen on television. Half the time, these dozen mechanical thoughts conflict with one another. They take the driver out and start their backswing thinking about stiff left arms, still heads, full turns, wrist cocks, or pronated hands. Without realizing it, they're doing anything possible to undermine their own game.

—BOB ROTELLA, *GOLF IS NOT A GAME OF PERFECT* (1995)

I try to hit the ball with the driver while the club head is traveling parallel to the ground; in other words, precisely at the bottom of the swing arc. If I fail to do that, I want the club head to be moving very slightly upward at impact. In both cases the ball will be hit forcefully forward, which is imperative for maximum distance. Any time you make a downward glancing impact with the driver you sacrifice distance by increasing backspin at the cost of forward thrust . . . In fact, teeing the ball low definitely encourages a downward rather than a sweeping hit. Thus, on most full drives I tee up so that the top of the club face is level with the ball's equator when the club is grounded . . .

One of the reasons I like to drive the ball high with a slight fade is the control this type of shot gives me in hitting specific targets . . . I always try to think positively in planning each tee shot by selecting a target to hit rather than an area to avoid.

—JACK NICKLAUS, *JACK NICKLAUS'*
LESSON TEE WITH KEN BOWDEN (1972)

Most golfers try to take too big a swing on the drive. I advise my students to shorten up the backswing and take it to ten o'clock. Keep the left arm level across the chest and make a good turn, properly shifting your weight from the right side to the left with a smooth follow-through toward the target. From the putter to the driver, less backswing and more through swing adds control.

—Marian Burke Blain, head professional, Seven Oaks, Colgate University, Hamilton, New York (2000)

Learn to hit up on the driver: Many golfers set up with the driver the way they do with an iron and then hit down on the ball. Instead, learn to sweep the ball off the tee by practicing the correct setup on an upslope. Place more weight on your right side, with the left hip bumped slightly forward and your spine tilted slightly to the right. Now take this "launch position" to the tee.

—David Leadbetter, "Hit it Farther, Straighter, Closer" in *Golf Digest* (2000)

When deciding your driving strategy, you have to start at the green and work your way back to the tee. Decide the kind of second shot that you want coming into the green on a par 4, for example. Know the pin placements and the contour of the green. If the pin is positioned on the left side of the green on a par-4 hole, play your tee shot to the right of center so that you will have a better angle when you hit your approach shot. For the average player, pin placements might not be a big deal. The average player just wants to get on the green in regulation. But planning still helps the high handicapper with strategy.

—Steve Friedlander, general manager and director of golf, Blackwolf Run and Whistling Straits, Kohler, Wisconsin (2000)

When I turned pro, my swing was much looser, and I had a definite control problem. I could lose it both left and right off the tee . . . The biggest adjustment I had to make was to take a shorter backswing . . .

When I do hit an errant shot, I've learned to take my medicine and get the ball back in play—most of the time. There are times, though—for example, if I'm 2 down with two to play and have to make a birdie—that I will try to hit the heroic shot. That's also part of what makes the game fun.

—TIGER WOODS, "THE LESSONS I'VE LEARNED" IN *GOLF DIGEST* (2000)

CHAPTER 7

DOWN THE FAIRWAY

Golf is a game of strategic angles and targets played over terrain that can range from windswept, treeless links-land courses festooned with randomly placed pot bunkers and snarly dune grass, to thickly wooded mountain courses with sharp elevation changes, uneven lies, and zany bounces. After the tee shot, as one heads down the fairway, the challenges of finding the best way to the target unfold. And with the best laid plans, there is the demand for execution—a four-iron draw shaped around a dogleg, a sweeping long iron off a pine needle lie, a downhill, side-hill seven-iron, a tricky little bump-and-run shot through a narrow opening to the green.

Bobby Jones ruefully noted: "On the golf course, a man may be the dogged victim of inexorable fate, be struck down by an appalling stroke of tragedy, become the hero of unbelievable melodrama, or the clown in a sidesplitting comedy—any of these within a few hours, and all without having to bury a corpse or repair a tangled personality."

One of the most notable features of Vardon's iron play was its beautiful cleanness. He just shaved the roots of the grass and made no gaping wound in the turf (and that was so, even in the shot singularly ill-named the "push-shot," about which industrious journalists wrote columns when Vardon was devastating the country). Down came the club hitting the ball first and going on to graze the turf, and away flew the ball starting low and then rising gradually to fall very dead from the undercut put on it. He played this shot often with a cleek and he played it with his iron; he had not a whole series of irons to play it with as his successors have today.

—BERNARD DARWIN, "VARDON'S METHOD" IN *THE DARWIN SKETCHBOOK* (WRITINGS FROM 1910 TO 1958)

Do not use a long club when a short one will answer your purpose better. It is better to be five yards short of a bunker than five yards nearer the hole, in it.

—HORACE HUTCHINSON, *HINTS ON THE GAME OF GOLF* (1888)

He tried to hit the ball with too much wrist and too little of anything else. Also, I fancied that his right elbow was not clinging to his side as it ought, but flying out from the body on the way down. At any rate, it was by trying to be very stiff and to keep that elbow under control that he checked the pestilence; but, for all I know, both the cause of the attack and the manner of its arrest were really quite other than those I have described.

—BERNARD DARWIN, "HOW TO CURE YOUR SHAN . . . ?" IN *THE DARWIN SKETCHBOOK* (WRITINGS FROM 1910 TO 1958)

Always use the club that takes the least out of you. Play with a long iron instead of forcing your shot with a short iron. Never say, "Oh, I think I can reach it with such and such a club." There ought never to be any question of your reaching it, so use the next more powerful club in order that you will have a little in hand.

—HARRY VARDON, IN *THE AMERICAN GOLFER* MAGAZINE (1927)

Many golfers now carry a mashie to the entire exclusion of the niblick; yet, though it be doubtful whether in the multitude of golf clubs there be wisdom, it is questionable if it is wise to discard the niblick altogether. For your mashie, for approaching purposes, should be essentially a weapon of balance, while your niblick, for digging purposes, should be essentially a weapon of weight. Your niblick should be heavy, to dig through obstacles; your mashie should be comparatively light, to pitch the ball dead.

—HORACE HUTCHINSON, "CLUBS AND BALLS"
IN *THE BADMINTON LIBRARY: GOLF* (1890)

How wise in him it was too to take his iron for the second at the seventeenth in the last round [of the British Open at Prince's], when he was growing rather shaky and knew it. In other rounds, he had been hitting the most generous seconds right home with wood, but this time his ball lay a little more right, the danger of the bunker was a little greater and his confidence was a little on the wane; so he took his iron and played for five. It is not every one who would have had so much self-control at that moment . . .

—BERNARD DARWIN, "GENE SARAZEN" IN *THE DARWIN
SKETCHBOOK* (WRITINGS FROM 1910 TO 1958)

The second shot is usually the shot that determines whether the player is to putt for a birdie or have to fight for a buzzard. If the target for his second shot is a small target with bunkers or other obstacles barring his path to the pin, the odds favor that chance that the player will be playing out of trouble with his third and having little chance for his par. But if, when he takes his stance for his second shot, the player is faced by the easiest possible route to the green, by a target that is big and wide, the chances of securing a par or birdie increase tremendously.

—CRAIG WOOD, "CRAIG WOOD TELLS HOW HE DID IT"
IN *THE AMERICAN GOLFER* MAGAZINE (1933)

One time at Chattanooga I hit a real pretty iron to the green, and danged if my ball didn't hit a bobwhite in the air and knock it dead. My ball stopped about a foot from the cup and I tapped it in. Only time I ever made two birdies on the same hole.

—SAM SNEAD, IN *THE SNAKE IN THE SAND TRAP AND OTHER MISADVENTURES ON THE GOLF TOUR* BY LEE TREVINO (1985)

The stance I favor for long irons, fairway wood clubs, and the driver is a closed stance, particularly for the fairway wood clubs and the driver. The reason is that this stance gives you more traction and balance. It enables you to strike the most powerful blow required to get the most out of those clubs. In order to get the real distance with them you've got to be firmly anchored.

Another reason for favoring this stance on these shots is that it enables you to turn your body more freely. Freedom of body turn permits you to lengthen the arc of your swing for the longer shots.

—BEN HOGAN, *BEN HOGAN'S POWER GOLF* (1948)

The good middle iron (five, six, seven) player can make well-positioned drives pay off. I like to open my stance a bit on these shots to get a freer, easier backswing movement. Aim for the big part of the green under normal circumstances and start back slowly, deliberately. The hands should get only a bit above shoulder height on a mid-iron shot. Power isn't the number one aim in this shot; direction is. And the shorter and more controlled the backswing, the straighter your shot. Experts keep the left heel on the ground in the backswing, although they do roll the feet over. Most weight should be felt on the inside of the right foot at this point.

The long-iron swing is a sweeping motion, rather than the downward action used for shorter clubs. First, play the ball forward, off your left instep. Then take a full pivot, or body turn as you swing back. The ball is contacted slightly on the upswing in a long-iron shot. As in every other golf shot except the sand explosion, it must be contacted first. But the swing path isn't down and through but "up" and through.

—ARNOLD PALMER, *THE ARNOLD PALMER METHOD* (1959)

Hitting from the rough:

1. Remember that the club should come into contact with the grass before it reaches the ball. Cock the blade a little open at address to allow for the tendency of grass to close the club face.
2. Grip the club firmly and hit the ball crisply.
3. Estimate the distance required, allowing for backspin and more roll.
4. In heavy rough, play the ball slightly back of the normal position. This will cause a sharper downswing.

—DOUG FORD, *THE WEDGE BOOK* (1963)

For all iron clubs, hit down and through the ball. In other words your club should contact the ball first, then the turf. Consequently, the lowest point in your swing will be a half inch to two inches in front of your ball. This causes the ball to adhere to the surface of your club face long enough to impart spin. The ball is being squeezed between your club face and the grass beneath it. The spin imparted is underspin, usually referred to as backspin. Backspin not only affects the ball when it lands but also in flight. When backspin has been applied the ball bores through the air more accurately.

—JULIUS BOROS, *SWING EASY, HIT HARD* (1965)

[On this shot] the ball flies low and long, probably with a slight fade. [Use] for long distance, especially into the wind, and when the fairway lie is excellent with the ball resting high on the grass.

Play the ball in the middle of your stance (except for an uphill shot, when it should be off the left heel). Swing slowly, bringing the club head back low to the ground. [Use a] complete backswing, start down deliberately. Try to sweep the ball off the grass, but get a feeling of hitting down on it slightly.

—BILLY CASPER, *GOLF SHOTMAKING WITH BILLY CASPER* (1966)

At address the club face must sit squarely and the arms and club and club shaft form a natural Y shape. If the lie is very grassy and the ball sits up well, play the ball several inches ahead of center. If the lie is tighter with less grass beneath the ball, position it just ahead of center. The contact is key to making good fairway wood shots . . . The swing is much the same as that for the driver with emphasis on roundness but brushing the ground rather than picking the ball off the tee.

—VIVIEN SAUNDERS, *THE GOLF HANDBOOK FOR WOMEN* (2000)

Underclubbing is most common in certain situations. You should be especially aware of the need for using more club in these cases:

1. When the air is damp . . .
2. Into a strong headwind . . .
3. Shooting to a raised green . . .

Often these shot-shortening conditions come in a combined form.

—TOM WATSON, *TOM WATSON'S STRATEGIC GOLF* WITH NICK SEITZ (1993)

The key to a good short shot is keeping a firm left wrist. There should be no break in the left wrist as you swing the club. The minute the left wrist turns over (left), or quits (right), you lose your accuracy. Think about hitting the ball crisply. Finish up with the back of your left hand toward the hole.

—AMY ALCOTT, IN *A WOMAN'S GOLF GAME* BY SHIRLI KASKIE (1982)

Never hit your irons as hard as you can. This is especially important for mid-to-high handicappers, who typically select a club expecting they're going to hit it perfectly. Instead, take one club more than you think you need and swing more easily. I don't do this as a rule because I'm on the range half my life.

But if I'm between clubs with trouble in front of the green, or a slight wind in my face, I'll take more club, grip down, and swing easy.

—HELEN ALFREDSSON, "PLAY YOUR 'A' GAME"
IN *GOLF FOR WOMEN* (2000)

I move the ball forward in my stance, adding loft to the club face, to hit it higher. As with the low shot, I make sure I square the club face to the target. Moving the ball up toward your front foot encourages a higher swing finish, and I strive to finish high with my arms. I also want to stay back with my upper body on the downswing.

Hitting the ball high, I select one more club than usual—a six-iron instead of a seven-iron, for example—and more than that into the wind, because I'll lose distance . . . Play the ball an inch closer to your body. If you're worried about hitting the ball high enough, set your left thumb straight down the shaft or even a little left of that . . .

—TOM WATSON, *TOM WATSON'S STRATEGIC
GOLF* WITH NICK SEITZ (1993)

Judging distance well and taking the right club are essential to good scoring . . . In order to improve, try to pass the flag on every single shot you play . . . To judge distance well, do not select the club to be used until you are right at the ball . . . A flag toward the back of the green probably looks closer to the back than it really is and may tempt you not to take enough club . . . Flags are not always uniform height. A tall flag can look easier than it really is; a small one can make the shot look shorter. Judge the distance to the green with people on it. Large bunkers can look deceptively close. Beware of undulations that appear just in front of the green. There may be 30 or 40 yards of hidden ground, tempting you to underclub. Very flat ground can be difficult to judge, with hidden ground and distances you just don't see. Tall trees look closer than they really are or may make a flag look very small and farther away. Try to judge distance with people in front of the green. If there is hidden ground you can often learn about the distance by watching them walk to the green and counting the number of paces they take.

—VIVIEN SAUNDERS, *THE GOLF HANDBOOK FOR WOMEN* (2000)

When you find that your ball lies in a depression, such as an old divot mark, don't panic. Unless the ball is deeply buried, you should be able to execute an iron shot that will bring practically the same result you'd get from a normal lie. To dislodge the ball from a depressed lie, your club head must be descending sharply as it comes into the ball. If the club head is not descending sharply it may stike the turf behind the ball or catch only the top part of the ball. You will achieve the upright swing if you retain more weight than normal on your left foot throughout your swing, especially during your backswing. The weight distribution to your left causes your club head to rise quickly on the backswing and descend sharply on the downswing.

—ARNOLD PALMER, *THE ARNOLD PALMER METHOD* (1959)

When playing a par-5 hole, think about where your approach shot to the green should ideally be. If you are a strong seven-iron player at a distance of around 130 yards, you should try to get into that range after your first two shots. If you hit a good tee shot, remember to leave your second shot in an ideal position. Too many average golfers think drive and then three-wood on par 5s, even though that might leave a more delicate approach shot than if they had used another club rather than [the] three-wood. I'm amazed at how many golfers mismanage par 5s.

—STEVE FRIEDLANDER, GENERAL MANAGER AND DIRECTOR
OF GOLF, BLACKWOLF RUN AND WHISTLING
STRAITS, KOHLER, WISCONSIN (2000)

Hitting the ball low is primarily a matter of ball position. I move the ball back in my stance. Moving the ball back reduces the effective loft of the club. Be aware that when you move the ball back you must square your club face to the target, because your normal club face position would now be open. I don't consciously adjust my weight distribution. This follows from the ball position. For a low shot I try to finish my swing low . . .

Play the ball an inch or so closer to your body on low or high shots or you'll hit the ball on the toe of the club.

—TOM WATSON, *TOM WATSON'S STRATEGIC
GOLF* WITH NICK SEITZ (1993)

When using long irons on the fairway, keep the same swing tempo and swing thoughts as you would use with shorter clubs. Try to hit down on the ball and don't be afraid of taking a divot. Keep the ball a bit forward in your stance and stand a bit farther away from the ball. The divot will be shallower as you make impact where your swing flattens out at the bottom of its arc. Relax; don't freeze up, relax.

—DOUG HODGE, PGA PROFESSIONAL, GRAYHAWK
GOLF CLUB, SCOTTSDALE, ARIZONA (2000)

In my opinion, fairway woods are more forgiving and easier to hit higher than long irons. The woods hold the greens more than three- and four-irons and are easier to use out of the rough . . .

First I look at the lie of the ball and the wind. Then I decide how far I want to hit the ball, and I make sure to check the green to see if it is hard and will cause the ball to roll or land soft. Before I play, I visualize the exact shot I want to hit and then take a practice swing. Then I go behind the ball and pick a spot three or four feet in front of the ball in line with my shot to help me aim.

Next comes the setup and shot execution. I always have a swing thought to keep my focus . . . Stay within yourself. Stay focused. Think positive. Take a deep breath and relax . . .

—LISELOTTE NEUMAN, LPGA TOUR PLAYER, "HOW TO HIT THAT FAIRWAY WOOD," IN *GOLF DIGEST FOR WOMEN* (2000)

Everything that happens from the tee to that 120-yard range is almost insignificant compared with what happens thereafter . . . A good golfer must not only accept the preeminence of the short game. He must learn to relish getting the ball into the hole, to love it as much or more than mere ball-striking . . . The threshold distance for an amateur might be 40, 60, or 80 yards, depending on his or her skills. Every player has to judge that individually. But inside your threshold distance, don't just go for the middle of the green and don't just try to get close. From inside your threshold distance, think about holing the shot.

—BOB ROTELLA, *GOLF IS NOT A GAME OF PERFECT* (1995)

On your approach shots take at least a club more and slow your swing down. Professionals, including Tiger Woods, hit three-quarter shots, rather than swing full force when hitting to the green.

—TOM SMACK, DIRECTOR OF GOLF, THE SAGAMORE GOLF CLUB,
BOLTON LANDING, NEW YORK (2000)

The lie of the ball always influences what club you choose. The lie is a primary influence on shotmaking and one that many golfers underestimate. It determines the trajectory and distance of your shot. The worse the lie, the more I'll tend to play the ball back in my stance. Playing the ball back and keeping my hands ahead of the ball through impact will produce a more descending blow and some solid contact . . . If the ball is in long grass that lies in the opposite direction of the shot I'm going to play, I'll consciously try to hit the ball harder. Conversely, if the ball is lying downgrain, I'll hit it easier.

So always examine closely the lie of the ball to determine what the ball is likely to do. This makes it much easier to choose the right club for the best results.

—TOM WATSON, *TOM WATSON'S STRATEGIC
GOLF* WITH NICK SEITZ (1993)

CHAPTER 8

AROUND THE GREEN: FROM FLOP SHOTS TO SAND BLASTS

As one approaches the hole, the muscles and nerves tend to tighten as the margin for error becomes smaller and the demand for deftness of touch becomes more pronounced. Even the most casual golfer can tell you that the vast majority of strokes that are taken will be from 60 yards in.

As Raymond Floyd, one of the great short-game players on the PGA Tour, relates in his book *The Elements of Scoring:*

> Once you become good at the short game, it transforms you as a golfer. A good short game greatly reduces the pressure to hit your long shots well: That fact alone can actually improve your ball striking. When you're playing well and feeling confident, a good short game allows you to be aggressive because you know you can recover from a lost gamble. When you're playing poorly, a good short game makes it easier to stay patient and weather the storm.

If your adversary is badly bunkered there is no rule against your standing over him and counting his strokes aloud, with increasing gusto as their number mounts up; but it will be a wiser precaution to arm yourself with the niblick before doing so, so as to meet him on equal terms.

—HORACE HUTCHINSON, *HINTS ON GOLF* (1886)

With regard to all approach shots, however, it cannot be repeated too often that the failing of the great majority of players is being short. For one shot that is past, you will see six that are not up. Therefore, when doubtful what club to take for your approach shot, it is a good rule to always take the longer of the two between which you are hesitating, for remember, you base your calculations on the assumption that you are going to hit the ball correctly. No accident is therefore likely to make the ball go farther than your expectation, while the accidents that may possibly curtail its distance are, alas! Only too many.

—HORACE HUTCHINSON, "ELEMENTARY INSTRUCTION: APPROACHING" IN *THE BADMINTON LIBRARY: GOLF* (1890)

A bunker or a trap . . . is supposed to be a place that calls for a stroke penalty, not a shallow dip where the golfer can walk in with iron or spoon to get 170 yards, or where anyone can use a putter. If I had my way there would be a troop of cavalry horses run through every trap and bunker on the course before a tournament started, where only the niblick could get the ball out and then out only by a few yards. I have seen a number of traps and bunkers that afforded better lies and easier strokes than fairways. This, of course, is ridiculous.

—CHARLES B. MACDONALD, AMERICA'S FIRST PROMINENT GOLF COURSE ARCHITECT, "WHAT MAKES A GOLF COURSE GREAT?: ONE OF AMERICA'S LEADING ARCHITECTS SPEAKS HIS MIND" IN *THE AMERICAN GOLFER* MAGAZINE (1924)

But it was in pitching, in all sorts of bunker shots, especially the more delicate ones, and in putting that he excelled. He had a fine stance on the green, comfortable and yet rocklike, and a velvety touch. It would hardly be possible to name a better putter day in and day out, but that which more than anything else at once fascinated the crowd and made him so formidable was his power of recovery . . .

Especially was he skilled in taking the ball cleanly out from a bunker, a shot needing immense confidence, since a grain or two of sand might ruin it. I shall never forget one such shot he played at the 15th hole at Sandwich . . . That bunker is a fairly deep one with a fairly steep bank, and many a stout-hearted player, however good the lie, would in this situation have played an "explosion" shot and made as sure as might be his five. Hagen took one good look at the ball, then flicked it out with exquisite precision close to the hole, and that as if it were the easiest shot in the world . . .

—BERNARD DARWIN, "WALTER HAGEN" IN *THE DARWIN SKETCHBOOK* (WRITINGS FROM 1910 TO 1958)

But Walter has his very good reasons for the change of clubs, and as he explains it himself, the use of three or four different tools actually tends to simplify the business.

It all depends on the portion of chip and roll he desires. If his ball is, say, 20 yards from the edge of the green, and the cup is pretty close to that side, Walter will take a mashie niblick so as to get more chip than roll, lifting the ball over the intervening fairway, or rough, or trap, and dropping it on the smooth green with the brakes on it, so the roll is curtailed.

If the proportion is fifty-fifty, he will take a deep-faced mashie; and if he is close to the edge of the green and the cup is well back, he will use a mashie-iron or even a mid-iron, giving the shot less chip and more roll.

But in every shot of this nature, and with every club, Walter hits the same way; a smart, crisp blow, the club just snipping the turf and taking the ball fairly in the back. That is the secret of simplicity in his chip shot. In place of varying the stroke to get more pitch and less roll, or vice versa, he varies the club to suit the situation—and hits the ball the same way every time.

—O. B. KEELER, "THE STYLE OF WALTER HAGEN" IN *THE AMERICAN GOLFER* MAGAZINE (1923)

Though born and bred at St. Andrews, where they play the run-up shot, I advocate pitching and stopping with the mashie. The Americans, among whom I recently spent three months, practice this shot in all their spare time, before or after matches. They know its value.

The way to stop a mashie shot is to give what we call in Scotland a "dunsh." This is done by bringing the head of the club under the ball, with the back of the left hand facing the flag. Underspin is thus imparted, without the ball being deflected. It drags forward a short way as the underspin pulls it up . . .

I do not know any shot more calculated to help the improver to take strokes off his handicap.

—SANDY HERD, "THE THREE TYPES OF PUPIL: WHICH ONE ARE YOU?" IN *THE AMERICAN GOLFER* MAGAZINE (1923)

In the hands of experts, the wedge has become a great shot-saver, but the experts make most things look easy; and when top-flight professionals admitted that the wedge technique did not come instantly to them, ordinary mortals had to beware . . .

The general misconception is to take it for shots of 80, 90, or even 100 yards, and to hit in order to get the distance. Used within the proper range and with a swing, it can become a precision tool. The best golfers make their wedge shots with the utmost deliberation, almost in slow motion.

—ENID WILSON, *A GALLERY OF WOMEN GOLFERS* (1961)

It is surprising how few people ever bother to experiment with the simple run-up, but those who do take the trouble rarely regret it. There is nothing complicated about it! The length of the stroke is controlled by the position of the hands on the shaft, for it follows automatically that when the hands are near the bottom of the grip, the stroke is restricted. Going down the grip is a detail that escapes many golfers, who try to control the distance by checking the force of the downswing as the club head nears the ball—this being one of the best ways of guaranteeing a fluff.

—ENID WILSON, *A GALLERY OF WOMEN GOLFERS* (1961)

First you must plant your feet firmly in the sand, to make sure you don't slip. Then you must lay your club face back until it is pointing straight to the sky. Aim to the left of the hole, keep your eye on the imaginary bottom of the ball, and hit hard. The shot must be hit hard to come off. A halfhearted swing will probably leave you still in the bunker, and you know the main idea of bunker play is to get out in one stroke. First, get out, and second, get as close as possible to the hole. But there is still another trick. Don't grip the club at all with the thumb and forefinger of your right hand. Let them lie loose on the grip, so the club can fit loosely in the circle formed by them. The shot is entirely a left-handed one.

—FRED MCLEOD, "THE KING OF BUNKER PLAY" IN
THE AMERICAN GOLFER MAGAZINE (1931)

A drive is nearly always a drive, and a five-iron shot just a five-iron shot. But a chip may be anything, and it rarely is the same thing twice. Especially over keen greens, a man must be a good judge of slopes, and the speed of putting surfaces; he must also be keenly appreciative of the effect upon the roll of the ball to be had from the lie of the ball, the loft of the club, and the trajectory of its brief flight.

—BOBBY JONES, *BOBBY JONES ON GOLF* (1966)

In taking your position to play the short irons the feet are fairly close together. The left foot is withdrawn slightly from the imaginary line parallel to the line of flight, forming the open stance. The left toe is pointed out and the hips have been faced slightly toward the objective. The weight is equally distributed between both feet. The knees are flexed and bent in toward each other slightly. This stance is used on short-iron shots because it enables you to keep your left side out of the way while contacting the ball and going on through the follow-through to the finish. The reason is that the swing is so short that it is impossible to take a full turn with the hips to accommodate the hands and arms with space to swing through . . .

In using the sand wedge to make a pitch shot all you have to do is hit a little back of the ball. This club is ideal for pitch shots because the blade has plenty of loft and the flange prevents the club blade from digging into the ground. When this shot is

gauged correctly and hit properly the ball should fly right up and give you the correct loft for a pitch shot to the green.
—BEN HOGAN, *BEN HOGAN'S POWER GOLF* (1948)

When it comes to chip shots it seems that practically every golfer has an inborn fear he won't give the ball enough loft. He wants to see that ball travel in a high arc, so he sets his weight back on the right leg and makes a jerky swing with his hands back of the club head at the moment of impact . . . To correct these faults, first make sure your left wrist is straight and on a line with the shot. Turn, when you swing, the key thing to remember is the hands, not the wrists. The backswing uses both hands evenly, with a certain amount of play in the wrists. So does the downswing. The hands lead the club head slightly. At impact you should feel yourself striking down and through the ball . . . The loft of the club head will supply all the loft you need.
—JOHNNY REVOLTA, IN *TIPS FROM THE TOP,* EDITED BY HERBERT WARREN WIND (1955)

If your ball has settled low in the grass, but still rests on grass expect a low-flying shot. Chip with a more lofted club to get height and to dig the ball out easily. Conversely, a ball that sits up high in the grass will be a "highflyer," so it's wiser to chip with a less lofted club to cut down the height . . . [If] the ball rests between grass, but still on bare ground: From this lie, stick with a straighter-face club, such as a five- or six-iron. Pop the ball out, by using a firm, sharply descending swing.
—ARNOLD PALMER, *THE ARNOLD PALMER METHOD* (1959)

The punch shot is used mostly in a crosswind or directly into the wind when you are from 30 to 50 yards from the green . . . It is vital that you keep your weight to the left side in hitting the punch shot . . . leaning a little bit in the direction of the target with your hands, well ahead of the ball (toward the target). The ball should be played a bit more toward the right foot than normal. The stance remains open, as with the normal wedge shot . . . A firm left arm and wrists drive the club into the ball and turf. This is reflected in the finish, which is very short.

—DOUG FORD, *THE WEDGE BOOK* [1963]

Never feel inhibited to experiment with different shots. You can start chipping little shots around the green with a pitching wedge and a sand wedge. These won't give you much roll. Then try using a seven-iron to see what the difference in the loft does to the roll the ball has.

If you have more green to work with, like a 30-foot roll, why not use a six-, seven-, or eight-iron? I firmly believe that when you have a lot of green to work with, like 30, 40, or 50 feet, the lower you can keep the ball to the ground, the more accurate your chip is going to be.

—AMY ALCOTT, IN *A WOMAN'S GOLF GAME*
BY SHIRLI KASKIE [1982]

I would prefer to have my ball 40 feet away from the hole in an ordinary sand trap lie than behind a bunker on good grass 90 feet away. Also, I would rather have a short explosion shot of 25 feet than a putt of 60 feet.

—PAUL RUNYAN, IN *THE WEDGE BOOK* BY DOUG FORD [1963]

Chipping from sand:

1. Use a six-, seven-, eight-, or nine-iron.
2. Chip only when there is no lip on the sand trap; [the] ball rests high on the sand, [the] hole is not close to the near edge of the green.
3. [The] ball [is] played on line slightly inside [the] left heel.
4. Make sure [the] club head strikes ball first.

—DOUG FORD, *THE WEDGE BOOK* (1963)

If you have difficulty lofting pitch shots, a steeper approach may help. Mid- and high-handicappers tend to swing the club on a relatively shallow path when pitching in an attempt to scoop the ball with their hands. Not only is a shallow swing path incorrect, so is the reasoning behind it.

But before changing your swing, change your mind about how a pitch shot achieves its height. Your job is to swing the club down into the back of the ball; the club's job is to use its loft to propel the ball into the air.

—PAUL MARCHAND, GOLF PROFESSIONAL AT
SHADOWHAWK GOLF CLUB, RICHMOND, TEXAS,
"NEW HEIGHTS" IN *GOLF MAGAZINE* (2000)

When playing short irons, keep the stance square—that is, parallel to the line of your shot. A common fault with short irons is to pull the ball left of target. The club head of a short iron is heavy and swings through fast. Golfers often slice to the right with the woods and pull to the left with the short irons. To remedy this fault, keep the club face of your short irons square at address.

—VIVIEN SAUNDERS, *THE GOLF HANDBOOK FOR WOMEN* (2000)

[A ball is under the lip of a bunker.] There's nothing too technical about this shot. You have to power the ball up and out. Brace your body with your front foot, anchoring it into the slope (provided the hill isn't too steep) so you don't lose your balance and fall. Make a powerful, shoulder-driven swing, accelerating the club head straight down into the sand just behind the ball. Forget the sand wedge and use a pitching wedge or a nine-iron for this shot because there's less bounce in these clubs. You want the leading edge to dig in, driving the ball up and out as quickly as possible.

—ANNIKA SORENSTAM, "DOWN AND UNDER"
IN *GOLF FOR WOMEN* (2000)

[A buried lie in the front lip of a bunker:] Unless the lie is really severe, the ball generally comes out high and lands softly. At address, tilt your shoulders and hips to mirror the upslope with your right shoulder much lower than your left. Preset your weight slightly into your left side. This minimizes lower-body action and promotes a descending blow, which pops the ball out. As with a basic bunker shot, shoulders and club face are ahead of the ball. Grip down for added control; your follow-through will be abbreviated.

[Downhill lie at the back of a bunker:] No matter what adjustments you make this shot is tough. Tilt shoulders and hips enough so that [the] left shoulder is below the right and 90 percent of your weight is on the left leg. Widen your stance for stability and play the ball just ahead of center. Open the club face as much as possible, and don't release (rotate) your hands at impact—you want to keep the club face open as long as possible. To avoid hitting the sand or bank on the backswing, set the wrists early and swing on a steep plane; this will also help add loft. Your hands should finish low, following the downslope.

—DONNA ANDREWS, LPGA PROFESSIONAL,
TO KAY COCKRILL, IN *GOLF FOR WOMEN* (2000)

Think of your long chips as approach shots you want to cozy up next to the hole. Place six tees in a small circle around a practice hole and hit chip shots that stop within this area. On the golf course, imagine this circle as your target for these shots. Stop your shots within the perimeter and you won't bungle these easy up and downs.

—CHERYL ANDERSON, LPGA TEACHING PROFESSIONAL,
IN *GOLF FOR WOMEN* (2000)

I often tell students to pretend the ball is sitting on a tee that's pushed all the way down into the sand. The idea is to look at the ball but to swing through the middle of the tee below it. This image encourages two things: getting the club head under the ball with consistent depth, and keeping the swing moving through the sand.

—EDDIE MERRINS, PGA PROFESSIONAL, "TEE TIME"
IN *GOLF MAGAZINE* (2000)

How to hit a chip: I use a putting stroke, but with a lofted club . . . The key to chipping is the setup . . . You want your stance to be narrow, about twelve inches from heel to heel, and open—pull your left foot back from the target line. Your shoulders should be open to the target as well. Then place about 80 percent of your weight on your left side. By moving your hands ahead of the ball, you encourage the downward strike that you need to make solid contact with the ball. Place the ball on line about two inches to the left of your right big toe. During your stroke, focus on the back of your left wrist. Your left wrist must stay flat and firm, as in putting.

—GARY MCCORD, GOLF FOR DUMMIES (1999)

Always putt if you can putt. Chip if you can't putt. Pitch if you have no other option from around the green. It is better to play on the ground rather than through the air in these situations. Our golf courses are Pete Dye designs. He designs green complexes to favor the lower shot as opposed to a shot coming in through the air. Most American golfers think you have to hit it high but height is something you don't always want. And, considering the turf and grass around the greens on these courses, it is not easy to get the ball up in the air.

—STEVE FRIEDLANDER, GENERAL MANAGER AND DIRECTOR OF GOLF, BLACKWOLF RUN AND WHISTLING STRAITS, KOHLER, WISCONSIN (2000)

All great short-game players have great imagination around the green. To become more creative in visualizing your options and to develop better judgment on shot selection, practice tossing balls underhanded to the hole. Experiment with different speeds and trajectories, from high and soft to low and running. Notice which trajectory you need, and where you have to land the ball, to allow you to get it close to the hole. Use the results as a guideline to select the club and type of shot that could give you the same results.

—DAVID LEADBETTER, "HIT IT FARTHER, STRAIGHTER, CLOSER" IN GOLF DIGEST (2000)

It is important to be skilled at bunker play, especially on our Raptor course, where the greenside bunkers are deep. When practicing bunker shots feel is the key. Aim left, open your stance, open the club face, take the club head outside and across the ball and hit from one inch to one and a half inches behind the ball. Take an aggressive shot in order to propel the ball with the sand exploding from the bunker.

—DOUG HODGE, PGA PROFESSIONAL, GRAYHAWK
GOLF CLUB, SCOTTSDALE, ARIZONA (2000)

One of the weakest parts of my game when I first came on the tour was my bunker play, especially from deep greenside bunkers to short-side pins. I've improved a lot since then . . . I position the ball toward my forward foot and concentrate on a spot behind the ball where I want the club to enter the sand. The closer to the ball, the more spin I can impart. The key is to weaken my left-hand grip. This lets me use my right hand aggressively. I can cock the club quickly, get the club face more open, and throw my right hand at the ball. The ball lands softly, with less roll.

—TIGER WOODS, "THE LESSONS I'VE LEARNED"
IN *GOLF DIGEST* (2000)

CHAPTER 9

ON THE DANCE FLOOR: PUTTING

In the old days players had to take the links as they found them; greens received no special attention, and it was a long time before anyone conceived the notion that greens should be mown or even rolled. Now, of course, we have manicured greens with multitiers, several hundred square feet of surface, a variety of grass types, measured speeds, and innumerable variables such as relationship to mountains, drainage, proximity to water, and the like. Golf gurus such as Dave Pelz have written tomes on how to putt, giving further credence to Willie Park's famous remark: "A man who can putt is a match for anyone."

In the days of the feathery ball, the golfer had two putters, a driving putter for playing low shots along the fairway, and a green putter for use near the hole. Today, most golfers carry only one putter but its use is not confined solely to the putting green. Its use off the putting green can be effective; it is then known as a Texas wedge.

—*THE ENCYCLOPEDIA OF GOLF*, EDITED BY DONALD STEEL AND PETER RYDE (1975)

There is a tradition (writes Colonel Fergusson) that she found means to convert herself into a golf ball for the express purpose of spoiling her political adversary's game. Can you conceive a meaner trick? Thus when a hole was about to be "halved" and a gentle touch with the putter was all that was wanted to hole out and so divide, her ladyship by rolling the eighth of an inch to one side, caused the hole to be lost!

—ANDREW LANG REFERRING TO LADY ASHTON,
THE "BRIDE OF LAMMERMOOR," "GOLF: ITS HISTORY"
IN *THE BADMINTON LIBRARY: GOLF* (1890)

Some men putt at the hole; others take as a guide a blade of grass, or something to catch the eye, just as the line between the ball and the hole, and very near the latter is on the whole the safer method. The great difficulty in the delicate operation of putting is to hit the ball quite true, and great secret of hitting the ball true is to keep your eye fixedly on it at the moment of striking . . .

Do not get into the habit of pointing out the particularly salient blade of grass which you imagine to have been the cause of your failing to hole your putt. You may sometimes find your adversary, who has successfully holed his, irritatingly shortsighted on these occasions. Moreover, the opinion of a man who has just missed his putt, about the state of that particular putting green, is usually accepted with some reserve.

—HORACE HUTCHINSON, *HINTS ON THE GAME OF GOLF* (1886)

Once upon the putting green the slowest party is safe from persecution for the time. According to the present law and practice, the putting green is a sanctuary; no man may drive into or molest a party on the putting green. You might as well shoot a partridge on its nest, or commit the terrible crime known to the law of Scotland as "hamesuckery," i.e., assaulting a man in his own house.

—LORD WELLWOOD, "GENERAL REMARKS ON THE GAME"
IN *THE BADMINTON LIBRARY: GOLF* (1890)

Putting greens are to golf courses what faces are to portraits.
—CHARLES BLAIR MACDONALD, *SCOTLAND'S GIFT—GOLF* (1928)

From a technical point of view, the most interesting part of his game is his putting, and I think it has been the most practically valuable. It is also the one which he declares he never practices. Nowadays many people try to putt in his method, but once upon a time it would have been deemed sadly heterodox. He holds the club almost at the top of the shaft, with both elbows considerably crooked, and seems to putt almost from his shoulders, and at least from his elbows.

—BERNARD DARWIN ON FRANCIS OUIMET, "FRANCIS" IN
THE DARWIN SKETCHBOOK (WRITINGS FROM 1910 TO 1958)

The fellow having the least distance to putt does the best putting.

The tournament experts in the last few years have been putting better because they have paid more attention to approaching and chipping that brings them into position for easier putts. They see to it now that they get straight-away or uphill putts rather than risky, difficult taps that must roll downhill or make a very accurate "borrow" from a side-hill location.

Consequently, when you hear tournament players talk about marvelous putting you probably are hearing only part of the story. The part about the approach shot is not often mentioned.

—HERB GRAFFIS, *ESQUIRE'S WORLD OF GOLF* (1965)

He devised the scheme of smaller holes on the practice course at Garden City, holes only a trifle larger than the ball. He practiced here for hours. When you can drop them steadily in a two-inch cup, one double the size looks like a keg.

—GRANTLAND RICE ON WALTER TRAVIS, "THE OLD MAN" IN *THE AMERICAN GOLFER* MAGAZINE (1920)

He was, I fancy, the first man who putted with the "reverse overlapping" grip, that is to say with the forefinger of the left hand riding on the little finger of the right. That is today the putting grip of Bobby Jones and Hagen and various other fine golfers; in fact, it may be called the orthodox grip recommended for putting by American professors.

—BERNARD DARWIN, "A RECOLLECTION OF WALTER TRAVIS" IN *THE DARWIN SKETCHBOOK* (WRITINGS FROM 1910 TO 1958)

A well-grounded putting technique is essential, of course, but you must have more than that. In theory, anyone who has learned to putt a ball successfully under a given set of circumstances should be able to repeat the performance over and over again without once missing, so long as the circumstances remain the same . . .

A good putt, the kind of long, curling, perfect putt that makes the gallery gasp, can only be the product of science and skill.

It means that the golfer who made it has studied out his shot beforehand, that he has made every bit of technical proficiency he possesses count to the utmost.

—JERRY TRAVERS, "THINK BEFORE YOU PUTT"
IN *THE AMERICAN GOLFER* MAGAZINE (1933)

The basic principle of good putting is to keep the blade of the putter square to the hole. When you talk turkey with a businessman you must look squarely at him during the conversation. It's the same in putting . . . Most of the time, when a golfer fails to take the putter back square to the target, the error he makes is "breaking" the wrists. This causes him to pull the putter off the line and eventually to cut the putt off to the right or yank it to the left of the hole. To correct this habit of breaking the wrists, I suggest placing the index finger of the right hand so that it extends directly down the shaft—behind the shaft. You can't break your wrists then, and the finger also serves as a fine guide in making the stroke.

—GENE SARAZEN, IN *TIPS FROM THE TOP*,
EDITED BY HERBERT WARREN WIND (1955)

The first thing needed for good putting is mental balance. This means mental and nerve control—coolness, lack of worry, a feeling of ease, and decision that isn't half guessing. Make some decision on the line and speed of the greens and then play it that way—right or wrong. You are almost sure to be wrong if you are still guessing as you hit the ball . . .

Have you ever noticed how often you hole a five- or six-foot putt with one hand when you are out of a hole? That means with the strain lifted you are relaxed and you let the head of the putter have its way without checking it or hurrying it. When golfers begin to miss short putts of two, three, and four feet it is usually because they are gripping too tightly, the sign of too much tension. Loosen the grip a little, try to pick out a more comfortable stance, and keep the swing smooth. This will often help a lot.

—WALTER HAGEN, "MY ANGLE OF PUTTING: SOME ADVICE FROM ONE OF THE GREATEST OF THEM ALL" IN *THE AMERICAN GOLFER* MAGAZINE (1929)

Croquet putting: A method of putting similar to that of striking a croquet ball, with hands separated on the shaft, legs astride the line of the putt. It was declared illegal in 1967 on the grounds that it did not constitute a golf stroke, to those who found it a cure to the shakes . . .

They also introduced a regulation governing the single shaft to the head of the putter, requiring a divergence of at least 10 degrees from the vertical. The croquet method called for a shaft set at right angles to the head.

—*THE ENCYCLOPEDIA OF GOLF*, EDITED BY DONALD STEEL AND PETER RYDE (1975)

On the putting green the mind can be a grave source of trouble. Begin to dislike the look of a putt, and the chances of holing it at once become less.

—JOYCE WETHERED, IN *THE QUOTABLE GOLFER*, EDITED BY ROBERT McCORD (2000)

Putting—a game within a game—might justly be said to be the most important part of golf. In almost every championship, or even in friendly matches, if the competitors are anything like evenly matched, the man who will win will be the one enjoying a definite superiority on and around the greens; for it is usually only on finishing a hole that a clear stroke can be picked up . . .

The most helpful single thing I was able to do to my putting stroke concerns the left elbow. I found that by bending over enough to produce a decided crook in the arms, and by moving my left elbow away from my body until it pointed almost directly toward the hole, I was able to create a condition of relaxation and easy freedom I could get no other way . . . The reason for the beneficial effect is that this location of the left elbow places the left hand and wrist under perfect control.

—BOBBY JONES, *BOBBY JONES ON GOLF* (1966)

I liked to begin with Chandler Egan's loose grip and relaxed position; I liked to feel this grip become a little firmer in the three smaller fingers of my left hand as the club started back; and then, to add a little crispness to the stroke, I liked to feel a tiny flick of the right hand as I struck the ball. I know of no better way of describing mechanics than to say that the left hand controls the path of the stroke and the alignment of the face, while the right hand supplies the touch—that nice adjustment of speed that rolls a long putt to the edge of the hole . . .

Walter Travis, probably the greatest putter the game has ever seen, always said that he visualized the putting stroke as an attempt to drive an imaginary tack into the back of the ball. I tried this conception and long ago found it to be a valuable aid in putting—to keep in mind the exact line upon which the ball should be started toward the hole . . . Having selected the spot and allowed the eye to follow the line back to the ball, it is not at all difficult to imagine the line continued through the ball until it emerges at a point on its back side.

—BOBBY JONES, *BOBBY JONES ON GOLF* (1966)

She putts with an upright, orthodox style, generally with an aluminum-headed putter. After studying the line intently and deciding which way the ball must go, Miss Price takes up her position and, when making the stroke, her body is absolutely still. It sounds simple enough to be able to putt without moving the body but surprisingly few people ever manage to do it. And those who succeed in standing still putt well.

—ENID WILSON, *A GALLERY OF WOMEN GOLFERS* (1961)

Many average golfers are better with a putter than they are with a chipping club. Yet, these same players will often refuse to putt from just off the green because they feel the "correct" shot from such a position is the chip. Let me say right here and now that the so-called correct shot in any situation is the one that will give you the best results. Never feel guilty about putting from off the green, if you feel the putter will give you the best chance for a successful shot.

—ARNOLD PALMER, *THE ARNOLD PALMER METHOD* (1959)

I follow the principles of gripping a putter just as I do the rest of my clubs, on the theory that this feels more normal. For many players this means the regular Vardon overlap grip. But for me it is a full ten-finger grip. I use this so-called baseball grip, in swinging all my clubs . . . The right hand should never "take over" the putting stroke . . .

My putting stroke is what I call a "law of average" move. That is, I will hit the ball solidly and on the line a high percentage of the time . . . The best term to describe my putting is "pop." My two principle theories are:

1. Try to always hit the ball with the club head accelerating at impact.
2. Try to hit the ball solidly. (If you do the first, it is easy to do the second.)

—BOB ROSBURG, *THE PUTTER BOOK* (1963)

Hitting a golf ball and putting have nothing in common. They're two different games. You work all your life to perfect a repeating swing that will get you to the greens, and then you have to try to do something that is totally unrelated. There shouldn't be any cups, just flag sticks. And then the man who hit the most fairways and greens and got closest to the pin would be the tournament winner.

—BEN HOGAN, IN *THE DOGGED VICTIMS OF INEXORABLE FATE* BY DAN JENKINS (1970)

In my style of putting, I never allow my left wrist to hinge or break after impact. I see to it that the left hand leads the stroke, so that my right hand never gets a chance to take over and, thus, close the blade of the putter on through the stroke. In this way I keep the blade accelerating way past the point of impact for a firm decisive stroke.

—ARNOLD PALMER, *THE ARNOLD PALMER METHOD* (1959)

Three physical characteristics of a green influence how and where a putt should hit:

1. The contour—the rises or dips of the green and the slope between the ball and the hole.
2. The type of grass—the character of its blades and direction in which it grows.
3. The speed of the surface—as determined by how recently it was mowed and current weather conditions.

—BOB ROSBURG, *THE PUTTER BOOK* (1963)

Everybody has a different problem putting. The best thing you can have is a quick left wrist. That makes you take the club head back on the inside. Most of your weight ought to be on the left foot for good balance. Another important thing is to keep both thumbs squarely on top of the grip for the right feel.

The feel of the club may be the most important thing of all. When you reach in your pocket for a coin the last thing that touches the coin is your thumb. You use it to roll out the coin. It's the most sensitive finger. That's why you grip the putter with both thumbs on top of the handle . . .

Take the club back on the inside, like opening a door, and then bring it forward. When you open a door, take it back slow. When you close the door, that's the way the putter should meet the ball.

—GEORGE LOW, IN *THE DOGGED VICTIMS OF INEXORABLE FATE* BY DAN JENKINS (1970)

Here's how to check grain and direction when you are facing a
long putt: Grain can be detected by looking closely at the
sheen of the grass. First, take a look at the line of the putt from
behind your ball. If the grass looks shiny, the grain is with you.
If it looks dark, then it is against you. If you can't tell, check
from the side. You might have a cross-grain to contend with.
Grain is more noticeable on seaside and mountain courses. It
will usually run toward the water and away from the mountains.

—BILLY CASPER, *GOLF SHOTMAKING WITH BILLY CASPER* (1966)

Avoid breaking down your left wrist on the putting stroke. Don't
cup your right hand or get wristy when you putt. Have a simple
swing thought and make a good stroke. Don't clutter your mind,
be positive. Make sure your eyes are lined up over the ball and
try to develop a feel for distance and distance control while you
are practicing your putting.

—RICK POHLE, HEAD PROFESSIONAL, TACONIC
GOLF CLUB, WILLIAMSTOWN, MASSACHUSETTS (2000)

Above all else, this [being positive] is the prime requirement
for being a good putter. It is a condition of the mind that is
developed and exercised like a set of body muscles. To be a
good putter, you must think of how you can make the putt—
not how or where you are going to miss it, which is negative
thinking. Develop the attitude that you can hole every putt.
This creates a supreme feeling of confidence in your ability to
do so. It pushes the negative thoughts out of your mind and lets
the positive thoughts dominate your mental attitude.

—BILLY CASPER, "SHORT GAME STRATEGY," IN *SECRETS
OF THE GOLFING GREATS*, EDITED BY TOM SCOTT (1965)

Straight downhill putts are usually easier to make than straight uphill putts . . . Gravity tends to focus the line of downhill putts, while helping uphill putts to diverge.

—DAVE PELZ, *DAVE PELZ'S PUTTING BIBLE* (2000)

It is important to spend time on the putting green gauging speed. Practice putting to the edge of the green without a hole. If you put extra weight on your front foot, that helps you to follow through. Don't just swat the ball around. Practice systematically. Practice easy uphill putts. Work on three-footers to get your shoulders rocking and take your hands out of the swing. Have a goal, such as making five three-footers in a row. The speed of our greens is usually 9 to 11 on the stimpmeter so it is important to develop a feel for speed.

—LANCE MCCULLOUGH, ASSISTANT PROFESSIONAL AND TEACHING PROFESSIONAL, CORDOVA BAY GOLF CLUB, VICTORIA, BRITISH COLUMBIA (2000)

On long putts, the biggest fallacy I see players falling for is the three-foot target. This is an imaginary circle with a radius of three feet and the hole at the center. Some teachers suggest a player facing a long putt should try to get the ball inside the circle. This makes no sense. Think about an archer or a pistol shooter. They shoot at an artificial target with a bull's eye and concentric outer circles. But no matter what the distance, they always aim for the bull's eye. It gives them the biggest margin of error. Even if they miss it, they're likely to hit something on the target. The same principle applies to putting. Always aim to make it.

—BOB ROTELLA, *GOLF IS NOT A GAME OF PERFECT* (1995)

If you have quick greens and you are hitting the putt downhill, if you putt the ball off the toe of your putter, the outer edge, you can stroke it normally. The ball will roll slower. If you line the putt up on the toe of your putter, the ball comes off much softer. It does work.

—NANCY LOPEZ, IN *A WOMAN'S GOLF GAME*
BY SHIRLI KASKIE (1982)

A smooth, slow stroke is needed when putting. Keep the club low to the ground, take it straight back and through. Crenshaw, Woods, Mickelson—the great putters are fluid back and through. A longer stroke is needed, not a short jab. A square line is the key in order to avoid closing or opening the blade. You have to practice a lot to be a good putter. It is a game within a game. The average golfer does not spend enough time practicing his putting.

—TOM SMACK, DIRECTOR OF GOLF AND
HEAD PROFESSIONAL, THE SAGAMORE GOLF
CLUB, BOLTON LANDING, NEW YORK (2000)

I said to him, "Forget about what your father's saying. Forget about what I'm saying. Forget about what Mark O'Meara is saying. Just go putt the way you want to putt. Don't listen to anybody."

—BUTCH HARMON TO TIGER WOODS IN EARLY 1999,
SPORTS ILLUSTRATED (2000)

I've always been an aggressive putter. During my junior golf and amateur days, I would knock it four or five feet past and drill it coming back. However, the greens on tour are faster and more undulating. Most of the time on tour you have to be "passively aggressive" . . .

The key is pace of stroke and pace of ball, controlled by a longer, slower stroke. When I'm rolling it well, my backstroke and forward stroke are almost identical in length. If one is shorter, it will not be my forward stroke; you don't want to decelerate . . . Enjoy a longer, slower stroke on long putts.

—TIGER WOODS, "THE LESSONS I'VE LEARNED"
IN *GOLF DIGEST* (2000)

CHAPTER 10

SCRAMBLING: TROUBLE SHOTS

The average or high-handicap golfer must wonder why golf television commentators are sometimes aghast when a Tour player bounces one off a tree, chili-dips one into the water or misses a green by several yards. For most of us, this is all in a day's work. In golf lore, Walter Hagen was one of the most notorious scramblers, yet he was very effective because he accepted the fact that he would hit imperfect shots.

The writer Grantland Rice noted in a 1925 issue of *Colliers* magazine:

> Golf is a game which can start a mental flurry in a second, but Hagen has won so many championships because in addition to fine physical skill . . . he has built up a philosophy which Fate can't overthrow . . . It takes an avalanche of accidents to make him sore. An earthquake would hardly leave him grouchy. He seems to be happiest when there's a hard battle ahead and he must come from behind to win.

Hagen noted in his biography, *The Walter Hagen Story,* published in 1956:

> I decided then that mental and physical relaxation during competition was the most valuable asset any golfer could possess. Concentrate on playing the best you can on each shot . . . if it's

a good one, that's fine. If it's bad, forget it. I expected to make so many bad ones anyway. I had to recognize that fact and aim to get the good ones where they counted most.

In the typical niblick shot the ball lies in a heel-mark or other cup in the sand, with the face of the bunker in front. To surmount this face, you must strike rather downwards some two or three inches behind the ball. The exact distance will depend on the height and nemesis of the cliff of the bunker, and the consistency of the sand. The looser the sand, and the higher and nearer the cliff, the farther you must aim behind the ball in order to make it rise straight enough off the club. I may safely say that this is the only stroke in golf in which you ought not to keep your eye on the ball. Your eye should be fixed on the exact spot at which you wish the niblick-head to cleave the sand.

—HORACE HUTCHINSON, *HINTS ON THE GAME OF GOLF* (1886)

The primitive condition of early links courses called for some unusual clubs, among them the track iron used for hitting out of cart tracks, and the baffling spoon, the most lofted of the numerous wooden clubs carried.

—DONALD STEEL, "LINKS COURSES: NATURE'S GIFT TO GOLF" IN *THE WORLD ATLAS OF GOLF,* EDITED BY PAT WARD-THOMAS, CHARLES PRICE, DONALD STEEL, AND HERBERT WARREN WIND (1991)

When the wind is with you, try a low tee. You will then find that a greater command is obtained over the ball. It will also rise high enough to add additional length which might be expected with the wind's assistance. The reasonableness of this should appear at a glance. A higher tee generally results in underspin being imparted to the ball, which is just what is not wanted in a following wind. By teeing low the underspin will not be so pronounced. The wind will then carry the ball in the air much farther than if it had, as billiard players say, "bottom" on it . . .

Take now the wind that blows from left to right. I do not believe in playing any tricks with the wind. I very much more prefer to correct an idea of its strength . . . There is no need to try to impart slice to the ball. The thing to do is to hit the ball truly, taking an aim some distance to the left, according to the wind's strength. The ball will go in the air for perhaps 150 or more yards without being appreciably affected in its course . . . As the momentum expires, what happens is this: The wind carries the ball over to the right into the middle of the fairway, or into the green. I am of course assuming that the drive has been correctly made. Any attempt to cut the ball in the act of hitting it, when the wind is blowing in this direction, can only have the effect of shortening the drive and exaggerating the "bend" of the shot when it finishes.

When the wind blows from right to left, you may attempt the pull shot as a means of gaining length. Here again I contend that it is only necessary to hit the ball clean and truly, taking the proper line to reap all the advantages the wind can give.

—TED RAY, "COMBATING THE WIND: CHANCES ARE
YOU ARE GOING ABOUT IT IN THE WRONG WAY"
IN *THE AMERICAN GOLFER* MAGAZINE (1924)

Fore! The golfer's traditional warning call when other players or bystanders are in peril of being struck by a ball. It also warns, or requests, others to get out of the line of play, or, less politely, encourages those in front to hurry. The usage probably derives from "Beware Before!," a military command mentioned by John Knox in the sixteenth century, warning troops to drop to the ground so that the guns might fire over them.

—*The Encyclopedia of Golf*, edited by
Donald Steel and Peter Ryde (1975)

The stars of the game sometimes give one the impression that they do considerable worrying over poor shots, but such is not the case. Hagen, for instance, is of the type who believes if a tee shot finds the rough the recovery will more than make up for the bad tee shot. He is willing to believe all shots cannot be played perfectly, and though he does play most of them fault-lessly, a ragged stretch of golf will not dampen his ardor, for he thinks in the end all things are evened up.

—Francis Ouimet, "At the Close of the Round:
Casual Observances on Some of the Many Phases
of Golf" in *The American Golfer* magazine (1923)

The hardest shot is a mashie at 90 yards from the green, where the ball has to be played against an oak tree, bounces back into the sand trap, hits a stone, bounces on the green, and then rolls into the cup. That shot is so difficult I have made it only once.

—Zeppo Marx, in "The End of the Hike: Details of Bobby
Jones' First Championship Victory" by Grantland Rice,
in *The American Golfer* magazine (1923)

A good player prays for wind every day, but he must not pray too earnestly.

—John L. Low (1928)

Gene [Sarazen] doesn't seem to care whether the ball winds up on the fairway or in the rough. He is the exception that proves the rule in my theory. But we must remember that Sarazen can play a shot out of the rough that no other living man can play. In fact he plays quite as well off rough ground as he plays off fairway. And if he misses the target with his second and lands in the bunker, again we find him the greatest of all bunker players. Sarazen is one in a million who needs no targets to shoot at for the reason that he probably will be putting for his par regardless of whether his shots from the tee to green have been played off fairway, rough, or concrete.

—MAXWELL STYLES, "CRAIG WOOD TELLS HOW HE DID IT"
IN *THE AMERICAN GOLFER* MAGAZINE (1933)

A headwind should be regarded as part of the golf course—just so many yards added to the hole.

—BOBBY JONES, *BOBBY JONES ON GOLF* (1966)

Skying the ball—A common complaint, especially from the tees or with the woods, is that the ball is popped high in the air. It comes from hitting too hard from the top of the swing, which causes the right shoulder to drop and the ball to be scooped skyward by the downward face of the club head. You correct this by slowing down on your downswing and not pressing the shot. If you really want to hit the ball a long way let the club head do the work. Never rush a shot.

—JOHNNY FARRELL, "CURING GOLF AILMENTS"
IN *SECRETS OF THE GOLFING GREATS*,
EDITED BY TOM SCOTT (1965)

The ability to recover well is of greater value to a woman golfer than it is to a man. She is obliged to use her wits to make up for lack of strength. Woman who make a habit of winning national titles . . . usually have their powers of recovery well developed.

—ENID WILSON, *A GALLERY OF WOMEN GOLFERS* (1961)

Yet he was no mere dreamer. On one course my companion hooked a ball into a neighboring garden, of which the owner was declared to be a fire-eater who allowed no balls to be retrieved but played with them himself. Then all the man of action in him awoke. He cast down my clubs as on lightening himself of his armour for a forlorn hope, took cover and crept, bending low, under the stone wall, climbed over the barbed wire, casting ever and anon wary glances at the silent house, and finally reappeared in triumph with the ball, sucking a wounded finger. Some day I shall be able to boast that a great man once carried my clubs.

—BERNARD DARWIN, "PORTRAIT OF A CADDIE" IN *THE DARWIN SKETCHBOOK* (WRITINGS FROM 1910 TO 1958)

I am going to take up here only some of the most obvious faults, or the most common ones that cause slicing. In every case the club head is pulled across the ball, but many things cause this fault. It may be that the left hand is not over far enough, or it may be that the right hand is gripping the club too tightly . . . So I suggest one of the first things to try out is to turn the left hand a trifle more over the shaft of the club and to ease up just a little with the grip of the right.

Another common fault is not turning the body and the left knee enough on the backswing. In place of this pivoting too many golfers pull away from the ball on the backswing. This nearly always forces them to pull across the ball on the downswing. It is necessary to correct slicing to see both the knee and the body turn far enough to prevent this pulling away.

Very often, also, slicing is caused by lifting the club in too upright a manner from the ball with the arms too stiff. To break up this fault start the club head back on a line inside the ball, on an arc on a line running through the ball towards the green. Don't let the club head get outside this arc.

—JIM BARNES, "HOW IS YOUR SLICE? SUGGESTIONS THAT
MAY ENABLE YOU TO ELIMINATE THIS TROUBLEMAKER"
IN *THE AMERICAN GOLFER* MAGAZINE (1922)

Mulligan: Slang for a friendly arrangement whereby a player has the option of a second drive from the first tee. It is largely an American habit. Not, of course, practiced in serious competition.

—*ENCYCLOPEDIA OF GOLF*, EDITED BY DONALD STEEL
AND PETER RYDE (1975)

Slicing—There are many reasons for a slice but there's only one way to do it and that's by bringing the club head across the ball—outside—and giving it a right-way spin.

Of the ways to slice, the number one enemy is getting the right side into the shot too quickly. And inside arc going back becoming an outside downswing is another fatal producer, and usually is caused by losing control of the shaft at the top of the backswing. A slice can also come from a left arm that isn't firm, and because it isn't firm, the right elbow strays . . . Many golfers slice too because they die on the shot, as the expression goes . . . An open stance with a wood or long iron will also produce a slice. Finally a slice can be traced to your grip. Be certain that your left hand is around the shaft and not slipping to the left so the palm is facing up. . . . Don't waste the power of that all-important left arm, hand, and wrist.

—JOHNNY FARRELL, "CURING GOLF AILMENTS" IN *SECRETS OF THE GOLFING GREATS*, EDITED BY TOM SCOTT (1965)

It has been my observation that beginners do most of the slicing—it takes an experienced golfer to develop a bad hook. It's true. During the first five years that a man plays golf he tries so many things to rid himself of a slice that he suddenly finds himself faced with the problem of losing a disastrous hook. But "hooking" is not confined to any one group of golfers, for the simple reason that a hook is most often the result of timing that has gone bad. And when the  expert golfer hooks a drive or a long iron it is generally spectacular because he trusts his swing. He bends back and lets go—and if his timing is off, however slightly—the hook that follows is sometimes unbelievable.

—JOHNNY FARRELL, "CURING GOLF AILMENTS" IN *SECRETS OF THE GOLFING GREATS*, EDITED BY TOM SCOTT (1965)

Rut Iron: An obsolete club used for striking the ball out of narrow ruts on rough tracks. It had a narrow round head so that it could get into all the smallest ruts.

—*THE ENCYCLOPEDIA OF GOLF*, EDITED BY DONALD STEEL AND PETER RYDE (1975)

When her name was called she did what most people do when they are apprehensive—she hurried and in her panic missed the ball altogether. A deadly hush ensued.

When she realized what had happened, her wits returned and with great presence of mind, she turned to her caddie and remarked in a peevish voice, as though he was to blame for her mishap: "How can I be expected to hit the ball when I do not know the length of the hole?!"

—ENID WILSON, *A GALLERY OF WOMEN GOLFERS* (1961)

Hitting against a wind accentuates the spinning action on the ball in all directions. Slices and hooks curve more and faster. By this same reasoning a hard hit ball with crisp backspin will sometimes climb higher in the air than usual and may drop short of the target. When hitting any shot against the wind I use a longer club, shorten up on my grip a little, hit a little easier, and let the wind stop the ball. The desire to hit harder against the wind should be suppressed. Swing normally. A following wind materially lessens the effect of all spins, so backspin cannot be expected to be as effective in controlling the flight or roll of the ball. Your ball will naturally carry farther and roll more. In this situation I play a shorter and more lofted club and play the shot higher.

—JULIUS BOROS, *SWING EASY, HIT HARD* (1965)

From fairway traps, play the ball a little forward of normal so as to contact it at the lowest point of the arc. Aim a little to the left of your target line because a slight fade will result from the fact that the body pivot is restricted . . . The pitching wedge shots from fairway or rough are played with that club when the experts want to slide more of the club under the ball and pop it up and on its way with high trajectory. Two points that the mentors stress in playing these shots are:

1. While keeping the left hand strong, don't hold the club so tightly that the wrist action is stiffened and
2. Stand and hit down so the leading edge of the club will come well under the ball and take the divot ahead of the ball.

—HERB GRAFFIS, *ESQUIRE'S WORLD OF GOLF* (1965)

The pushed ball, which flies off line to the right, does not spin; it was hit in that direction by the angle of the club face at impact. A push will generally fly in a straight line to the right; whereas the slice starts straight and then curves. The pulled ball, which is like the push although it flies to the left, is again the fault of the angle of the club face at impact. Lastly we have the topped shot, caused by the club striking the ball above its middle half or just below the middle with the leading edge of the club.

—JULIUS BOROS, *SWING EASY, HIT HARD* (1965)

When you need a relatively long shot from a moderate rough, play the ball in the middle of your stance. Take a square stance and align your body parallel to the line of flight with your hands slightly ahead of the ball. Aim the club face slightly to the right of the target because the grass may interfere with it, causing the club face to close at impact. You can expect a lower, long-running shot.

—SHIRLI KASKIE, *A WOMAN'S GOLF GAME* (1982)

[On a long-iron tee shot] the ball flies relatively low. [Use] whenever a low shot is required, as into a wind or through a crosswind, or under overhanging branches; also from elevated tees on par-3 holes within long iron or four-wood range.

Play the ball just forward of the center of the stance. [The] stance should be narrower than with woods, square to the interior line. The grip is especially firm. Use an upright, unhurried full swing; don't lunge on the downswing. Hit the ball first, take a small divot in front of the original ball position.

—BILLY CASPER, *GOLF SHOTMAKING WITH BILLY CASPER* (1966)

Topping—The best mechanical manner to avoid topping is to take a full, easy swing and play the ball well back toward the middle line. This minimizes the possibility of "picking up" the body and also cuts down the chances of taking your divot first and bouncing the club head into the ball for a topped shot. Remember, the driver should be taken after the ball is hit. The ball actually is pinched against the ground as it is struck first and is on its flight when the divot is taken. When you see that your divot is in the back of the ball, you know you are playing the shot too much off your left foot.

—SAM SNEAD, *SAM SNEAD'S BASIC GUIDE TO GOOD GOLF* (1961)

A classic case occurred in the 1974 English Open Amateur Stroke Play Championship at Moortown, when Nigel Denham, from Yorkshire County, had his adrenaline flowing as he approached the 18th green directly behind the Moortown clubhouse . . . Pumped up, he stroked his iron shot well over the green. The ball struck a path, took a long bounce up some steps, and rolled directly through an open door into the clubhouse. The clubhouse was not out of bounds at the time . . . The setting has a preciousness of its own; here is a player lying two in the bar, facing a difficult shot in the presence of a crowd of drinking competitors lined up at the clubhouse bar, some of whom might be celebrating, while others would rather forget . . .

He walked over and opened the window, returned to his ball, and after a few practice swings, gently lined his shot through the open window. It rolled onto the green and came to rest about twelve feet from the hole. Even his barside adversaries were forced to compliment him.

He concluded his remarkable performance by making the putt for an extraordinary par.

—GEORGE EBERL, *A GOOD WALK SPOILED* (1992)

Sidehill Lies—If the ball is higher than the feet, simply shorten your grip on the shaft. If it is lower than your feet, take a longer grip on the shaft.

When the ball is on a lower plane the difficulty is that you have a tendency to reach for the ball. The best means of dealing with the problem is to bend slightly at the knees to make certain that you keep most of the weight on the heels so you don't fall into the shot. You must stay down throughout the swing or you will top the ball. Also, take your stance slightly closer to the ball than usual.

When the ball is higher than the feet, balance is your main problem. So, in addition to shortening your grip on the club, take your stance slightly farther from the ball than usual and keep your weight on the balls of the feet. If you do this you will not fall away from the shot as you swing.

—SAM SNEAD, *SAM SNEAD'S BASIC GUIDE TO GOOD GOLF* (1961)

There are several reasons that golfers shank shots, but a very common one occurs on the backswing. If you take your club back too much "inside" the target line, around your body, you will be likely to return it along a path that forces the club head "outside" the ball. The result will be that the club's shaft, instead of its face, strikes the ball. If you shank shots, I suggest you try taking the club back more along the target line— straighter back from the ball. This will encourage your returning the club face squarely into the ball.

—ARNOLD PALMER, *THE ARNOLD PALMER METHOD* (1959)

One of the most common trouble shots where the wedge is indispensable is from the taller grass that borders the fairways . . . Even from short rough, when the blade of the wedge—or any other club—comes into the grass before contacting the ball, the grass will tend to wrap itself around the club head. This closes the blade at impact. To compensate for this tendency, which varies greatly depending on the strength and length of the grass, I just cock the blade a little open at address and thus have it a bit open at impact.

This opening of the face is especially necessary for a high shot from rough when I want as little roll as possible on the ball after it lands.

—DOUG FORD, *THE WEDGE BOOK* (1963)

If a ball comes to rest in dangerous proximity to a hippopotamus or crocodile, another ball may be dropped.

At a safe distance, no nearer the hole, without penalty.

—LOCAL RULE, NYANZA CLUB, BRITISH EAST AFRICA, 1950, IN *A GOOD WALK SPOILED* BY GEORGE EBERL (1992)

The downhill lie—Here the weight is mostly on the left leg and you have a tendency to slice. I prefer a closed stance to counteract the slice and the right knee is bent slightly for balance. The ball should be played slightly back of the center line. You will have a tendency to slice so aim a bit to the left of your objective.

In playing the downhill lie, you should use a club with more loft. This is due to the fact that you have trouble getting the ball into the air because the natural roll of the downhill position offsets some of the loft of your club. . . . Let the club do the work and don't try to "lift" the ball. The club will do the job if you give it a chance.

The uphill lie—On the uphill lie, the ball is placed slightly back from the line to the left heel. Due to the weight being mostly on the right foot, you may have a tendency to hook. Therefore, aim slightly right of your objective and open your stance the least bit.

Don't worry about getting the ball up in the air. The natural slope of the hill will help get the ball into the air, probably even more than you desire. It is a good rule to use the club with less loft than you would ordinarily, say a five instead of a six, because of the automatically imposed elevation of the shot.

—SAM SNEAD, *SAM SNEAD'S GUIDE TO GOOD GOLF* (1961)

Hardpan is solid baked ground that could be likened to a sidewalk or a roadway . . . From hardpan it is usually smarter to use a club without a definitely flanged sole—one that will cut under the ball instead of bouncing . . . It is vital to hit the ball before, or at the same instant as contacting the ground.

—DOUG FORD, *THE WEDGE BOOK* (1963)

When the ball is above your feet the tendency is to pull or hook to the left. To adjust, simply aim more to the right of the target. Also check to see that your club can clear the ground in a practice swing.

When the ball is below your feet the tendency is to push the ball, or slice. To adjust, simply aim more to the left of your target. Make sure that you are standing close enough to the ball so that you won't top it, and make a special effort to stay down with the shot.

In an uphill lie the tendency is to pull the ball and hit short of your target. To adjust, use at least one club stronger than usual for the distance and possibly more if the grade is severe. Keep your weight to the left side and play the ball a little farther forward in your stance. Aim slightly to the right.

In a downhill lie the tendency is to fade the shot to the right and to skull on top of it. To adjust, aim to the left and let the ball fade. Play the ball slightly back of center in your stance and stay down with the shot, following the contour of the ground.

—GARY WIREN, *GOLF* (1971)

Weather and wet ground conditions invariably produce "flyers"—shots that travel farther but bite less quickly than normal, due to reduced backspin caused by moisture on the ball and club face. One obvious way to counteract this is to take less club, but a more sophisticated and reliable way is to fade the ball into the green. The extra height and spin resulting from a straight out-to-in cutting action will generally counterbalance the effects of a wet ball and club face.

—JACK NICKLAUS, *JACK NICKLAUS' LESSON TEE*
WITH KEN BOWDEN (1972)

You need lofted woods to get out of the rough. I use a two-iron and a five-wood. In high rough I almost always take my five-wood. I'm strong as female golfers go. But I'm much better out of long grass with a wood than I am with an iron. I want to get out of the rough and still get some distance. So I go with a lofted wood.

—JUDY RANKIN, IN *A WOMAN'S GOLF GAME*
BY SHIRLI KASKIE (1982)

Ball below feet:

1. Take grip on end of shaft.
2. Club face squared to line of flight.
3. Club head enters sand one inch behind ball.
4. Stay "down" on shot until finish.

Ball above feet:

1. Aim slightly to the right.
2. Club face laid back (opened) slightly.
3. Grip down on club to accommodate fact that ball is closer to hands.
4. Ball played on line slightly inside left heel.
5. Club head enters sand one inch behind ball.

—DOUG FORD ON HOW TO HIT OUT OF BUNKERS,
IN *THE WEDGE BOOK* (1963)

Landing in divot holes distresses many golfers more than it need. There are basically two ways to overcome the problem. The first, to be adopted when you can run the ball onto the green, is to play a punch shot—ball back, club face square, hands ahead of the ball at address and impact, early pickup, three-quarter swing, firm downward hit, no rolling of wrists until well beyond impact. Number two, essential when the ball must fly to the target, [is to] move the ball forward, open the club face, take a full swing and hit hard with the right hand through impact—again taking care to roll the wrists until the ball is well on its way.

—JACK NICKLAUS, *JACK NICKLAUS' LESSON TEE*
WITH KEN BOWDEN (1972)

A typical trouble shot at Seven Oaks is a punch shot out of the trees. I advise that the golfer take the club back to a three o'clock position and follow through to nine o'clock to execute this shot. The main thing is to make solid contact and have good tempo. And it is important to take your medicine and get the ball back in play rather than trying to hit a heroic shot. Hit the shot you know you can hit, not what you think you can hit in this situation.

—MARIAN BURKE BLAIN, HEAD PROFESSIONAL,
SEVEN OAKS, COLGATE UNIVERSITY,
HAMILTON, NEW YORK (2000)

For pitch and chip shots from rough around the green, I set my sand wedge on the toe at address, especially on heavy U.S. Open–type rough. I raise my hands to set the club on its toe. It's easier to get the ball up in the air. There's less bounce in play with the sand wedge setting on its toe and the face stays open through impact easier . . . Play the shot with firmer wrists. Your results should be more reliable.

—TOM WATSON, *TOM WATSON'S STRATEGIC GOLF*
WITH NICK SEITZ (1993)

After an errant drive, when playing our desert courses, you are in luck if you are in a position to hit the ball off hardpan rather than losing it in the underbrush. Treat this hardpan shot in a way similar to a fairway bunker shot. Keep the lower body still, make contact with the ball first and take a conservative route in order to get the ball back into play.

—DOUG HODGE, PGA PROFESSIONAL, GRAYHAWK
GOLF CLUB, SCOTTSDALE, ARIZONA (2000)

To vary your distance you need to be able to control one set distance in the first place! Learn a basic bunker shot of about twelve paces. Short bunker shots: When aiming to hit about eight yards, shorten the swing and slow it down. Aim about two inches behind the ball and do not touch the sand with your club head. Medium bunker shots: When going for about 20 or 25 yards, use a splash shot with a square rather than open club face. Look closer to the ball—about two inches—and take less sand. Longer bunker shots: With a longer bunker shot from a perfect lie, just aim to hit the ball cleanly. From a poorer lie, hit the ball and then the sand. Take enough loft to negotiate any lip.

—VIVIEN SAUNDERS, *THE GOLF HANDBOOK FOR WOMEN* (2000)

Make sure you play the wind, don't let the wind play you. Don't swing hard when hitting into the wind. Play under control, because the ball won't go that far anyway. Club selection is important. Use one or two extra clubs. Shorten the backswing and swing more easily.

—PAUL PARKER, HEAD PROFESSIONAL, BUFFALO DUNES
GOLF COURSE, GARDEN CITY, KANSAS (2000)

When it comes to the game of life, I figure I've played the whole course. I've been struck with lightning and I've managed to make a few million dollars, although I never reached the eighth grade in school. There are certain special things in this world and right at the top are drivers and wives. I know. I've had three of each.

And from all this experience I've learned that a good driver is a helluva lot harder to find than a good wife.

—LEE TREVINO, *THE SNAKE IN THE SAND TRAP AND OTHER MISADVENTURES ON THE GOLF TOUR* (1985)

Two common mistakes are made when a golfer tries to play out of a pot bunker. The golfer doesn't hit the proper entry point when he hits the sand and the club does not go deep enough into the sand. Most players hit too far behind the ball. Hit the sand two or three inches behind the ball. Keep your weight on your left foot. Make certain you open the club face enough and hit the ball forward, not up. Do not try to scoop the ball. In this way your club will penetrate the sand more deeply and you will get a better result.

—FRED GRIFFEN, DIRECTOR OF GRAND CYPRESS GOLF ACADEMY, ORLANDO, FLORIDA (2000)

What about tight lies that can test you? You're on bare ground or in a divot or on pine needles. Or on dormant Bermuda over the winter. Play the ball back of center in your stance and hit it with more of a descending blow.

For this particular swing, I like to picture a good follow-through before I play the shot, with the swing continuing through the ball. I find I get better contact. From tight lies the ball will fly lower and tend to run more.

—TOM WATSON, *TOM WATSON'S STRATEGIC GOLF* WITH NICK SEITZ (1993)

CHAPTER 11

TOOLS: EQUIPMENT

The tools of golf have evolved in interesting and sometimes comical ways. In the days of the feathery ball (first referred to in writing around 1620), the golfer used two putters, a driving putter for playing low shots along the fairway, and a green putter for use nearer the hole. The ball evolved from stone to wood to the feathery, then to the gutta percha, which became common around 1848. In 1898 the rubber-core ball was patented by Coburn Haskell and replaced the gutty soon thereafter. The golf ball has become more supersonic ever since.

The earliest golfers used one club, but by the fifteenth century clubs evolved for special purposes. The play club, the forerunner of the driver, was one of the earliest specialty clubs, used for hitting balls off the tee and from level lies on the fairway. In many respects the ball dictated club design. When the rubber-core ball was introduced, harder woods were required for clubs that had previously been made of pear or apple.

As golf become more popular in the twentieth century, clubs and balls were mass-produced rather than handcrafted. After World War I hickory-shafted clubs were gradually replaced by steel-shafted clubs and, more recently, high-tech materials have become the norm. By the 1930s golfers were carrying as many as twenty-five clubs. Now the USGA and the Royal and Ancient limit the number of clubs to fourteen for use in official competition.

Harvey Penick, the noted golf instructor, believed that the most important clubs in the bag are the driver, the putter, and the wedge. Ben Hogan thought the same. Penick explains in his bestseller *Harvey Penick's Little Red Book:* "My reasoning is that you hit driver fourteen times in an ordinary round. But on the same day, you may have twenty-three to twenty-five putts that are outside the 'gimme' range but within a makeable distance."

For most of the four or five hundred years of golf history the player's equipment consisted only of clubs and balls, often just one of each. He wore what might be called his everyday clothes, including smooth-soled shoes. His clubs, if he had more than one, were carried loose under his arm or that of his caddie. He had no protection against the weather. He or his caddie teed the ball on a pinch of sand, and the score was kept by comparing the number of shots he had taken with those expended by his opponent.

—*THE ENCYCLOPEDIA OF GOLF*, EDITED BY
DONALD STEEL AND PETER RYDE (1975)

Baffy: A hickory-shafted wooden club manufactured in the days of the feathery and gutty ball. It roughly corresponds to the modern four- or five-wood.

—*THE ENCYCLOPEDIA OF GOLF*, EDITED BY
DONALD STEEL AND PETER RYDE (1975)

Nowadays the array of wooden clubs is commonly much curtailed. The "baffy," with which the golfer of old used to approach the hole, is now replaced by the lofting iron—much to the detriment, as the old golfer is so fond of telling us—and truly telling us, may be of the turf of the links, from which the iron skelps up such divots. The practiced iron player is always ready with the retort that men overuse the baffy now because they cannot play the iron.

—HORACE HUTCHINSON, "CLUBS AND BALLS"
IN THE BADMINTON LIBRARY: GOLF (1890)

Irons: The earliest types were crude-looking "Garrick" irons. They were deep in the blade and were used to hack the old feathery ball from rough places such as tracks and ruts. Hence the rut iron and the track iron. Then came the cleek with the advent of the gutty ball, which Allan Robertson realized could be easily adapted to use with irons; the niblick, introduced by Tom Morris for pitches; and the mashie, of which J. H. Taylor was the master. The mashie was the equivalent of a modern five-iron.

It was the Americans who developed the more lofted irons, the wedges. These suited their conditions better. With the adoption of steel shafts, however, matched sets of irons became the fashion; players now carried more than just a jigger, cleek, mashie, and niblick, and numbers replaced names.

—THE ENCYCLOPEDIA OF GOLF, EDITED BY
DONALD STEEL AND PETER RYDE (1975)

There are eleven implements of the game, the most important of which is the ball. This is made of gutta percha, and is painted white. It weighs about two ounces, and is just small enough to fit comfortably into the holes dug in the ground. Still it should not be so large that it cannot be taken out with ease. The other ten implements are the tools of the players. Their names are as follows: the playing spoon, long spoon, mud spoon, short spoon, baffling spoon, driving putter, putter, sand iron, cleek, and track iron. Each of these is about four feet long, the entire length of which in general consists of a wooden handle. The head is spliced on and may be either metal or wood. The handle, as a rule, is made of hickory covered with leather.

—HORACE HUTCHINSON, "CLUBS AND BALLS"
IN *THE BADMINTON LIBRARY: GOLF* (1890)

There is every reason to believe that the golf ball is obedient to the laws of dynamics rather than to your modest impassioned prayers or imprecations. Any good effect that can ensue from giving vent to the feelings must therefore be purely subjective. If profanity had an influence on the flight of the ball, the game would be played far better than it is.

—HORACE HUTCHINSON, *HINTS ON THE GAME OF GOLF* (1886)

He liked the old ball, which required clean and perfect hitting; he dislikes the new one, which he thinks enables many an imperfect hitter to "get away with it."

—BERNARD DARWIN ON HARRY VARDON'S PREFERENCE FOR THE
GUTTA PERCHA VS. THE RUBBER-CORE BALL, IN *THE
DARWIN SKETCHBOOK* (WRITINGS FROM 1910 TO 1958)

Cleek: A shallow-faced, hickory-shafted iron with loft roughly corresponding to the modern two-iron. Used in the days of the feathery and gutty ball to control long shots.

Spade mashie: An obsolete hickory-shafted iron a little stronger than a mashie niblick. It corresponds roughly to the modern six-iron.

Mashie: An obsolete hickory-shafted iron club with approximately the loft of a five-iron. As with other old golfing terms, it is linked with Scottish domesticity. The mashie does not resemble the instrument used for mashing potatoes, but it took its name from its effect on the ball when entrusted to unskillful hands.

Niblick: An old-fashioned iron club with more loft than a mashie. Used mainly for recovery play and pitching.

Jigger: An obsolete iron club with a narrow blade. It has no equivalent in the modern set but had roughly the loft of a four-iron and was mainly used for recoveries from bad lies and for chipping.

—*THE ENCYCLOPEDIA OF GOLF*, EDITED BY
DONALD STEEL AND PETER RYDE (1975)

The feathery was never a reliable ball. It was usually ovoid or oblate rather than spherical, and this affected its passage through the air and particularly its behavior on the ground. Wet weather not only made it heavier and less manageable, but combined with wear and tear, it rotted and broke with predictable results. An unkind cut with an iron club or collision with a sharp stone could cause irreparable damage. For these reasons, and also because the slow and tedious process of manufacture made it expensive, only well-to-do golfers could afford to buy the feathery and the less fortunate players had to be content with old balls or improvised substitutes. But this ball, with all its faults, lasted until 1848, when the peculiar properties of a Malayan elastic gum called gutta percha came to the notice of golfers . . .

The gutty had many advantages over the feathery including consistency of flight and roll, but the most important were cheapness and durability.

—*THE ENCYCLOPEDIA OF GOLF*, EDITED BY
DONALD STEEL AND PETER RYDE (1975)

Nowadays, in addition to balata, balls made of surlyn, lithium, and titanium are available. Modern balls tout varied dimple patterns, multiple layers, and other features that attempt to impart a certain trajectory, greater accuracy, and better feel, as well as the ever-popular maximum distance allowed under the Rules of Golf established by the USGA. According to Appendix III in the rules, the overall Distance Standard says that a ball "shall not cover an average distance of carry and roll exceeding 280 yards plus a tolerance of 6 percent." That means that no golfer should be able to average more than 296.8 yards with his or her best poke.

—GARY McCORD, *GOLF FOR DUMMIES* (1999)

How your clubs can help you—Properly fitted clubs are the only part of improved golf that anyone can buy . . . No other game is as exacting as golf in that so many specifications must be met to make a precision fit of implement and player.

—TOMMY ARMOUR, *HOW TO PLAY YOUR
BEST GOLF ALL THE TIME* (1953)

. . . A club should be so balanced that the head may be felt. But that doesn't mean it has to be heavy. Most real hitters prefer light clubs. The slow swingers like heavy clubs as a rule.

—STEWART MAIDEN TO O. B. KEELER, "THE MOST COMMON FAULTS" IN *THE AMERICAN GOLFER* MAGAZINE (1922)

Center shaft: A club with the shaft inserted in the middle of the head instead of the heel. The idea came from America at the turn of the century in the shape of the "Schenectady" putter used by Walter Travis in winning the 1904 British Amateur Championship.

—*THE ENCYCLOPEDIA OF GOLF*, EDITED BY DONALD STEEL AND PETER RYDE (1975)

The center-shaft putter is usually of an upright lie. It is amazingly effective from short distances. When the ball lies two yards or less from the hole, it is comparatively easy to keep the putter swinging on line with the hole. But this upright position is sometimes embarrassing to a free swing for a long approach putt. It is this difficulty, I believe, that has been largely responsible for the almost complete disappearance of the Schenectady and Travis models.

—BOBBY JONES, *BOBBY JONES ON GOLF* (1966)

The heavy bunker iron was one of only four types of iron used with the feather ball. Irons became more refined and more specialized in the gutta percha period when wood faces were used to cushion the shock of hitting the hard gutty ball. Later, scoring patterns, sometimes of rubber, were applied to club faces in attempts to achieve control. The continuing search for a lofted club to get under the ball produced the L. A. Young sand wedge in the 1920s . . . Gene Sarazen developed the straight-faced sand wedge with a heavy sole to allow it to move through the sand. He first used it in 1932, but its full impact was not until after World War II.

—DONALD STEEL, "THE EVOLUTION OF CLUBS AND BALLS" IN *THE WORLD ATLAS OF GOLF*, EDITED BY PAT WARD-THOMAS, CHARLES PRICE, DONALD STEEL, AND HERBERT WARREN WIND (1991)

For some reason the rank and file of women golfers treat their clubs poorly and put them away without ever wiping them down. Woods, whose varnish was chipped away years ago, repose with a covering of mud; irons similarly embellished have the stains of countless shots, and last season's grass, stuck in their grooves. Their grips are usually in a deplorable state—loose and shiny . . . This neglect seemed to indicate a state of mind in which there is no rapport between the owners and their clubs, rather as if there is a state of rancor. Why bother to look after implements that have turned sour on their wielders?

—ENID WILSON, *A GALLERY OF WOMEN GOLFERS* (1961)

The weight of driver that you will find best suited to your style of play must necessarily very hugely depend upon the speed of your swing. A slow swinger will incline to compensate for the want of velocity by the increased in weight. The thing to be aimed at is a balance between the two—not such weight as to make your natural swing drag; nor, again, such lightness that

your natural strength is in part wasted, or the swing for a
moment checked by the concussion of the ball . . .

—HORACE HUTCHINSON, "CLUBS AND BALLS"
IN *THE BADMINTON LIBRARY: GOLF* (1890)

Hickory: The wood from which the shafts of golf clubs used
to be made. It was replaced by steel (legalized by the Royal
and Ancient in 1929). Bobby Jones won all his championships with hickory-shafted clubs, including 1930, the
year of the Impregnable Quadrilateral. With hickory
shafts golf was a different game. They had torsion:
When swung they would twist as well as bend. They
could also be trimmed by sandpapering to give
exactly the sort of feel a player wanted . . .

—*THE ENCYCLOPEDIA OF GOLF*, EDITED BY
DONALD STEEL AND PETER RYDE (1975)

It would take a book to analyze all the feel and performance
nuances resulting from various combinations of shaft length
and flex and grip and head weight. Basically, however, the
stiffer the shaft, the greater the golfer's chance of delivering the
club face accurately to the ball, and thus the greater the percentage of his shots in play, and the more flexible the shaft, the
greater the potential club-head speed and thus the greater the
golfer's distance. But, when you get down to the practicalities,
the determining factors in selecting clubs must be your own
strength, swing tempo, and feel.

—JACK NICKLAUS, *JACK NICKLAUS' LESSON TEE*
WITH KEN BOWDEN (1972)

The importance of perfectly fitted clubs has been referred to as the governing factor in hitting the ball well. Teaching authorities have estimated that the 85 shooter wastes at least three shots a round because he doesn't know how to play the course and four shots a round because he uses the wrong clubs . . .

Most golfers haven't any idea of the loft of club faces or clubs and think that a five-wood, for example, has much more loft than, say, a three-iron. But the fact is that the five-wood loft is 21 to 23 degrees in leading manufacturers' lines and the three-iron has a 23-degree loft, sometimes slightly more.

The lie of the club varies according to the loft or the club face and the length of the shaft, with the 62-degree lie and 36-inch shaft about medium for the eight-iron and a 54-degree lie with 42- or 43-inch shaft regarded as standard for a man's driver. Whether the woods and irons should have standard, flat, or upright lies; what flexibility of shaft the clubs should have; the swing weight (the proportion of weight in the head compared to that in the shaft and the grip); whether there should be a slight hook or slice built into the assembly of the head and shaft; the grip sizes, and other specifications mean more than the average golfer realizes.

—HERB GRAFFIS, *ESQUIRE'S WORLD OF GOLF* (1965)

Every player should be fitted for clubs and not assume that he or she needs a standard set. I've played golf with hundreds of professional athletes, and most times they've shown up with standard-length clubs. Most of the tall guys were hunched over the ball, in very bad posture, and couldn't consistently make a good solid hit.

—SAM SNEAD, *THE GAME I LOVE* (1997)

The amount of confidence you have in your ability to play a particular club should also be given some consideration when you are selecting a club to make a shot which appears to be difficult. You can substitute a club you favor for the correct club to be used on a particular shot only if your favorite is quite similar to the correct club in the loft of its club face.

—BEN HOGAN, *BEN HOGAN'S POWER GOLF* (1948)

A drive which carries 200 yards in the air when the ball is 71 degrees Fahrenheit would carry 185 yards at 32 degrees. (This supports the practice of changing balls each hole in cold weather and substituting one that has been warming in the player's back pocket.)

The best combination of club weight to produce maximum distance can only be determined by personal experience in hitting balls. A larger-shafted driver (up to four inches over the 43 inches for men), however, would give one an advantage in distance without significant loss of accuracy.

Putters weighted at both the toe and heel have less chance of hitting errant putts when they stike the ball an off-center blow.

—GARY WIREN, *GOLF* (1971)

In selecting and using your wood clubs it would be well for you to remember that sometimes a player can change club heads without getting into difficulty, but generally speaking he is asking for trouble when he changes the shafts. The reason is that the flex and the weight of all shafts are different and they have a direct effect on the swing.

—BEN HOGAN, *BEN HOGAN'S POWER GOLF* (1948)

Clubs to avoid: My suggestion if you don't have a great deal of time for practice and are able to play only once or twice a week, or even less, is to eliminate the number one driver, the number two wood or brassie, and the two- and three-irons.

In their place obtain a one and one-half–wood and a five-wood, a four for two trade which will pay great dividends on your scorecard. The 100 shooter makes too many mistakes with the driver, which can be an instrument of Satan if you aren't swinging just right. A lot of duffers, feeling that the brassie is easier to handle, will use the number two wood off the tee. What they are forgetting is that, barring a precision swing, the face of the brassie is too shallow for use off a wooden tee . . . The brassie is also a dangerous fairway club unless you have a practically perfect lie.

—SAM SNEAD, *SAM SNEAD'S BASIC GUIDE TO GOOD GOLF* (1961)

The "bounce" or "ride" in a wedge keeps the club head from digging deeply into the ground when a descending blow is struck. The flanged sole makes the club "ride" below the surface without digging as deeply as would the straight-faced nine-iron.

—DOUG FORD, *THE WEDGE BOOK* (1963)

Start using the lofted woods, the five and seven, regularly in your game. You'll be a better player. I believe only women with handicaps of nine and under (scores in the low 80s) should ever use a two-iron. It is such a difficult club to use. Anyone over a 16 handicap (scores around 90) shouldn't be using a three-iron . . . Pitch out the three-iron. Put in a seven-wood. Nowadays there are five-woods and seven-woods that play just as well as the long irons for any average player.

—SALLY LITTLE, *A WOMAN'S GOLF GAME* (1982)

The degree of loft of a club face is the main factor in the distance attainable with that club. As a rule, the lower the number of the club, the lower the loft of the face—and the further it will hit the ball . . . If you add length to the club, the shaft becomes whippier and the head feels heavier. If you shorten a club, it becomes stiffer and there usually is less feel to the head. Smaller women golfers are best advised not to have their clubs shortened for this reason. It is easier just to grip further down the club.

For the average woman golfer, the ideal full set is a driver (one-wood) and three-, five-, and seven-woods; three-, four-, five-, six-, seven-, eight-, and nine-irons; a pitching wedge and sand wedge; and a putter.

—VIVIEN SAUNDERS, *THE GOLF HANDBOOK FOR WOMEN* (2000)

The average golfer golfs to get exercise and avoid problems. Don't add another problem by having unrealistic expectations and buying $800 to $1,500 worth of equipment without careful consideration. If you buy expensive equipment off the rack, you are likely to be frustrated if you can't improve. I'll loan you the clubs during lessons, until you develop realistic expectations.

—PAUL PARKER, HEAD PROFESSIONAL, BUFFALO DUNES
GOLF COURSE, GARDEN CITY, KANSAS (2000)

Buy clubs with the correct thickness of grip. In theory a thick grip encourages a slice to the right and a grip which is too thin will encourage you to hold the club too tightly or to hook to the left. With the correct grip the fingers of the left hand just barely touch the pad of the left thumb without digging in.

Make sure grips are put on correctly with any line or mark perfectly square to the club face. Grips are generally not perfectly round, but egg-shaped. If incorrectly fitted, you may find difficulty in holding the club face square and returning it squarely to the ball.

—VIVIEN SAUNDERS, *THE GOLF HANDBOOK FOR WOMEN* (2000)

Ten Questions to Ask When You Buy Clubs

1. Do you have a club-fitting program?
2. What's the price of club-fitting?
3. What shaft length do I need in clubs?
4. What lie angle do I need for my clubs?
5. What grip do I need?
6. What material—leather, cord, all-rubber—do you recommend for my grips?
7. What kind of irons should I buy—investment cast, forged, oversized, or cavity back?
8. Should I use space-age materials like boron, titanium, or graphite in my shafts? Or do I go with steel?
9. What type of putter should I use: center-shafted, end-shafted, or a long putter?
10. If you are going to buy new clubs, ask the pro if you can try them for a day.

—GARY McCORD, *GOLF FOR DUMMIES* (1999)

The sand wedge is an important club on our courses. The average to high handicap player should use a sand wedge with lots of bounce (e.g., a big flange). The better players might use a sand wedge with low bounce. Also, they should use a lob wedge (normally a 60-degree wedge) to handle tight lies in the desert.

—DOUG HODGES, PROFESSIONAL, GRAY HAWK GOLF CLUB, SCOTTSDALE, ARIZONA (2000)

There are more options now than ever when choosing equipment. Most manufacturers have custom fitting, which the golfer should take advantage of. You can put tape on the face of the club, go to the range, and have your swing analyzed. The person fitting you determines where the hands drop, the lie of the club and other factors. For example, the correct lie of the club will better enable you to follow the target line. Don't adjust your swing to the club, select a club to fit your swing. There is only a slight charge for this service and, if you buy clubs, you are usually not charged for the service at all. It is not a good idea to just buy a set of clubs off the rack.

—TOM SMACK, DIRECTOR OF GOLF AND HEAD PROFESSIONAL, THE SAGAMORE GOLF CLUB, BOLTON LANDING, NEW YORK (2000)

CHAPTER 12

GRACE
UNDER PRESSURE

It is truly amazing how great golfers can execute shots in the most difficult circumstances, especially in major championships under extreme pressure. One of the greatest golf champions is Jack Nicklaus, not only because he won twenty major championships, including two U.S. Amateurs, but because he was a gracious loser having finished second nineteen times in majors and fifty-eight times in his PGA Tour career.

In the 1966 British Open at Muirfield, Nicklaus needed a par on the final hole, a 427-yard par-3, to win. After hitting a one-iron off the tee, he recalls his thought process as he set up for a critical three-iron approach shot:

> Adrenaline makes you want to powder the ball, and it promotes that tendency in the muscles. As I set up for the fade—club face slightly open, body aimed a little left—I lock on the word "smooth." My target is the center of the green. The impact feels magical; as solid a strike as I've ever made . . . Resist the tendency to play too quickly under pressure and give yourself extra thinking time when your adrenaline is gushing hardest. The urge is to go with your instincts and take less club on approaches, but then you have to meet the

ball squarely for the shot to succeed. Smoothness with plenty of club is usually a better strategy.

Nicklaus won the 1966 British Open, his first, by one stroke with his two-putt par 4 on the final hole.

Now, in golf there is no such stimulus, and the mind has to be goaded into attention and action by laborious and incessant iteration of mental formulae dinned into the memory and repeated over and over again. (I know a man who repeats to himself six rules every time he takes a driver in hand and addresses the ball.) . . . As a matter of fact most of the difficulties in golf are mental, not physical; are subjective, not objective; are the created phantasms of the mind, not the veritable realities of the course.

—ARNOLD HAULTAIN, *THE MYSTERY OF GOLF* (1908)

As long as there are so many tournaments treading on one another's heels, there will, we may be sure, be very few challenge matches. It is a pity and something has gone out of the game on account of it, but nobody can blame the players . . . It was a very different matter in old days when roughly speaking a challenge match was the only way.

—BERNARD DARWIN, *THE DARWIN SKETCHBOOK* (WRITINGS FROM 1910 TO 1958)

Of course in every match your ultimate success will depend largely upon the terms on which you have arranged to play, before starting. The settling of these conditions is sometimes a nice matter, needing all the wisdom of the serpent in combination with the meekness of the dove. At such times you will perhaps be surprised to hear a person, when previously you believed to somewhat overrate his game, now speaking of it in terms of the greatest modesty.

—HORACE HUTCHINSON, *HINTS ON THE GAME OF GOLF* (1886)

When a hole is being keenly contested, and you look as though you are having the worst of it, try not to appear pleased when your opponent makes a bad stroke or gets into serious trouble, however relieved or even delighted you may feel. It is human nature to feel the better for your opponent's mistakes in a crisis of this kind, but it is not good manners to show that you feel it. And however well you may know your friend, it is not half so funny as you think it is to laugh at such a time or shout out that you rejoice. It is simply bad taste, for your opponent at the time is suffering from a keen sense of disappointment, and is temporarily quite unable to appreciate jokes of this kind. He is inclined to think he has been mistaken in you all along; and that you are much less of a gentleman and a sportsman than he imagined.

—HARRY VARDON, *THE COMPLETE GOLFER* (1905)

In the first case, one can see how easy it is to throw a chance away by not trying hard from start to finish, for one never knows that the other competitors may not be doing equally indifferently. The second instance is an excellent one of the principle, "Never give up trying." By following it you cannot possibly lose anything, and you may gain.

—HAROLD HILTON, *MY GOLFING REMINISCENCES* (1907)

Sir Walter's favorite strategem was the reverse approach—when faced with an easy shot, he pretended to be racked by doubts. He'd study the lie; he'd walk ahead to survey the green; he'd finger his clubs uncertainly; he'd shake his head, he'd address his ball and back away to change clubs. Then he'd drop one dead to the pin. The gallery would go wild and his opponent would be shaken.

But on an impossible shot The Haig would whip out an iron without hesitation and blithely swing away—also dropping dead to the pin. The gallery, appreciating the immensity of the feat, again would go wild. The opponent, who could appreciate it even more, would begin to wonder whether he was playing man or fiend—a fiend who could get supernatural help.

—ARTHUR DALEY, IN *THE NEW YORK TIMES* (1954)

One always feels that he is coming from something without knowing exactly what or where it is.

—BOBBY JONES ON CHAMPIONSHIP TOURNAMENT PRESSURE, *BOBBY JONES ON GOLF* (1966)

This factor is competitive instinct, which I believe to be more highly developed in Walter Hagen than in any other modern golfer. Walter Hagen never steps on a golf course except to win whatever match or competition he may be engaged in . . . He plays to win, and to win as decisively, as crushingly, as over-whelmingly as he can. A friendly match with Walter Hagen is a match all right—but he will beat you if he can, and as much as he can.

—O. B. KEELER, "THE STYLE OF WALTER HAGEN" IN *THE AMERICAN GOLFER* MAGAZINE (1923)

I always used a lot of strategy and psychology and it often paid off. I used it on them all. I set up shots the way a movie director sets up scenes . . . to pull all the suspense possible from every move. I strutted and smiled. I hooked and I sliced into rough off the fairways, but how I clobbered that little white ball when the chips were down, the gallery tense, and my opponent either overconfident or sick with apprehension. Sure, I grandstanded. But don't get the idea I was merely being amusing and brassy. To me that stuff was all part of my game. It helped fluster my opponent as much as it delighted the gallery . . . and was equally important in releasing the tension from my game.

—WALTER HAGEN, *THE WALTER HAGEN STORY* (1956)

That Hagen had an overpowering effect in match play on some of his opponents was clear enough. His demeanor towards them, though entirely correct, had yet a certain suppressed truculence; he exhibited so supreme a confidence that they could not get it out of their minds and could not live against it. They felt him to be a killer and could not resist being killed. He had a very shrewd eye for their weaknesses and, strictly within the limits of what was honest and permissible, he would now and then exploit [it] to his own advantage.

—BERNARD DARWIN, "WALTER HAGEN"
IN *THE DARWIN SKETCHBOOK*
(WRITINGS FROM 1910 TO 1958)

Figures are the things that matter more than anything else. At the end of the round there is a prolonged and terrifying succession of accountancy. Although matches are played, and holes are won, lost, and halved, the emphasis is inevitably on the total sum of strokes made during the round . . . With the

Americans it is the score that counts; with us [the British] the handicap is important.

—ENID WILSON, *A GALLERY OF WOMEN GOLFERS* (1961)

It is something like that, something like a cage. First you are expected to get into it, and then you are expected to stay there. But, of course, nobody can stay there. Out you go—and then you are trying your hardest to get back in again. Rather silly, isn't it, when golf—just golf—is so much fun?

—BOBBY JONES TO BERNARD DARWIN, "JONES RETIRES FROM BATTLE"
IN *THE DARWIN SKETCHBOOK* (WRITINGS FROM 1910 TO 1958)

On the golf course, a man may be the dogged victim of inexorable fate, be struck down by an appalling stroke of tragedy, become the hero of an unbelievable melodrama, or the clown in a side-splitting comedy—any of these within a few hours, and all without having to bury a corpse or repair a tangled personality.

—BOBBY JONES, IN *THE DOGGED VICTIM OF
INEXORABLE FATE* BY DAN JENKINS (1970)

I know the feeling of standing on a tee with real fear in my heart, the match slipping away and the club feeling strange and useless in my hand, and yet I have fortunately been able to laugh at myself for the absurdity of such intense feelings and the perversity of one's own thoughts.

—JOYCE WETHERED, IN "BOBBY JONES AND JOYCE WETHERED
PLAY THE OLD COURSE" BY S. L. MCKINLAY
IN *THE GLASGOW HERALD* (1957)

The only resource one has to fall back on is to try to understand and develop a philosophy which will cope with them [nerves], and here experiences will naturally differ. I know perfectly well the two qualities which have helped me most: the first is honesty with oneself and the other is a sense of humor. We have to recognize our weaknesses, and unless we realize them and refuse to make allowances for them they will catch us out every time in a crisis. When, however, we have learned them all and recognized that we are going to suffer from them always, it is worth a great deal to be able to feel amused by our own peculiar idiosyncrasies.

—JOYCE WETHERED, "COMPETITIVE GOLF"
IN *THE AMERICAN GOLFER* MAGAZINE (1931)

I twice had the frightening experience of seeing him come to the very edge of malice in fierce outbursts that neither he nor I understood. I was afraid for him, for I had seen him flushed and shaking in a rage of sudden anger, then drained white a moment later in sudden fear of the nearness of evil. In a sense, I shared his deep inner struggle to overcome what, with his intellect he knew to be ignoble. He knew well that he was poisoning himself with anger, that he must find the inner strength to rise above it . . .

Once he had achieved actual maturity by overcoming this disturbing and dangerous element of his nature, Jones became the most "balanced" person I have ever encountered in sport, a man who had achieved a rare harmonious unity of the inner self and outer self which had formerly been at war.

—AL LANEY, "GETTING TO KNOW BOBBY JONES"
IN *FOLLOWING THE LEADERS* (1968)

My turn to be the fodder of Glenna's ability came rather abruptly. It was my first meeting with her, and a great fear arose within me. The same fear haunts any new competitive golfer—that of having to match your shots against someone with better ones. You fear your cannot do your best, unless she is having an off day. Under a strain of this sort, I went to the course that afternoon and discovered it was possible to play very well with such turmoil within me. I won that match on the 19th hole. Naturally, I shall never forget it, but, what is more important, I shall not forget the consideration shown me by Glenna that day. She knew how nervous I was, but, rather than take advantage of it she honestly made an effort to get me over it. She is the type of golfer who prefers to match shots with you rather than see you mentally upset to the extent that you are incapable of playing good golf shots.

—VIRGINIA VAN WIE, "LEARNING HOW TO COMPETE"
IN *THE AMERICAN GOLFER* MAGAZINE (1934)

Fight! Fight! Fight! Why is that always preached to a young golfer? After all, if you hold the majority of the good cards, you stand a fine chance of beating Cuthbertson at bridge. My theory is this: If you perfect your golf shots, your opponent will need more than an unfriendly attitude to defeat you.

—VIRGINIA VAN WIE, "LEARNING HOW TO COMPETE"
IN *THE AMERICAN GOLFER* MAGAZINE (1934)

If you're going to be a victim of the first few holes, you don't have a prayer. You're like a puppet. You let the first holes jerk your strings and tell you how you're going to feel and how you're going to think.

—BOB ROTELLLA, *365 ANECDOTES AND LESSONS* (1997)

Putting affects the nerves more than anything. I would actually get nauseated over three-footers during my prime. And there were tournaments when I couldn't keep a meal down for four days. Missing a short putt is about the most humiliating thing in the world because you're supposed to make it.

—BYRON NELSON, IN *THE DOGGED VICTIMS OF INEXORABLE FATE* BY DAN JENKINS (1970)

Stroke play—or medal play, as it is otherwise known—is generally considered to be the most testing form of competition in golf. Play each shot as it comes and eventually the ball will drop in the hole at the 18th . . . [Some] dos and don'ts of stroke play:

- Don't become boastful if things are going well . . .
- Do remember that a bad start does not mean a bad round . . .
- Put the score out of your mind until the match is over . . .
- The only form of forward thinking you should do is to plan each hole as you get to it . . .
- See where the flag is and plan your drive carefully . . .
- Don't choose the club until you get to the shot . . .
- Don't take unnecessary risks . . .
- If you make a mistake, put it out of your mind as quickly as possible.

—VIVIEN SAUNDERS, *THE GOLF HANDBOOK FOR WOMEN* (2000)

I feel sorry for rich kids now. I really do. Because they're never going to have the opportunity I had. Because I know tough things, and I had a tough day all my life and can handle tough things. They can't. And every day that I progressed was a joy to me and I recognized it every day. I don't think I could have done what I've done if I hadn't had the tough days to begin with.

—BEN HOGAN, IN *HOGAN* BY CURT SAMPSON (1996)

What a spectacle it was to see Hogan hit every full shot like a god. To watch him putt like an expectant father on his third of coffee.

—CURT SAMPSON, *HOGAN* (1996)

No one was in the room with Hogan at the time, excepting his six-year-old son, who was playing on the floor. His wife and two other children were in an adjoining room when they heard the shot, and rushing in, they found Hogan on the floor with a smoking revolver by his side . . .

—ARTICLE ABOUT THE SUICIDE OF NINE-YEAR-OLD BEN HOGAN'S FATHER, CHESTER, IN *THE FORT WORTH RECORD* (1922)

There is a normal tendency when playing under unusual pressure to increase the firmness of your grip. This is bad because a grip that is too firm encourages a jerky swing, and a jerky hurried swing is especially harmful in tight situations when you need the best, smoothest swing you can muster. When you feel pressure, be it on the tee or on the green, relax your grip. Don't get sloppy about it, just relax a little in your hands.

A relaxed grip will in turn ease tension in your wrists and forearms. You will be more likely to take the club back smoothly and put yourself in position for a smooth, unhurried downswing.

—ARNOLD PALMER, *THE ARNOLD PALMER METHOD* (1959)

A lot of guys are afraid to make a putt. By that I mean they're afraid to win a tournament, especially a big one. I try to tell myself all the time that I'm a good putter. I try to psych myself into believing I can make anything. But most of us, we like to bleed about putting badly and hope that a good streak will sneak up on us. It's all superstition, I suppose.

—DON JANUARY, IN *THE DOGGED VICTIMS OF INEXORABLE FATE* BY DAN JENKINS (1970)

When facing a hazard, focus your attention sharply on your target, not the hazard.

—BOB ROTELLA, *365 ANECDOTES AND LESSONS* (1997)

The press still considers me one of the most laid-back athletes since Babe Ruth. That's supposed to be a criticism, but I consider it a compliment because I think being carefree on the course is one of the secrets of scoring well consistently. I'm not saying you should whistle "Summertime" while you're hitting shots. But I do think that when you're carefree, you're relaxed; and when you're relaxed, you swing more freely. All of which means you are going to generate maximum club-head speed on drives. On irons, you'll be less apt to steer the shot, which is one of the most common faults among club-level players.

—FRED COUPLES, *TOTAL SHOTMAKING* (1990)

The difference is that when you guys get in tournaments, the likelihood is that you'll lose your concentration on four or five shots every round. Over a four-day tournament, even if every lapse costs you just one stroke, that's sixteen to twenty shots a week, and that's the difference between being the leading money winner and losing your card . . . Over a career, losing concentration once in a while can mean lots of strokes.

—TOM KITE, IN *GOLF IS NOT A GAME OF PERFECT* BY BOB ROTELLA (1995)

Even if you don't start out on tour seeing things this way, you soon learn that your opponents aren't really the other players but yourself and the golf course, in that order. As golf involves no physical interchange between participants, you and the playing field are the only two things you can do anything about . . .

—JACK NICKLAUS, "MY FAVORITE PLACE TO PLAY" IN *GOLF MAGAZINE* (1997)

I couldn't figure it out. My marriage was fine, my kids were healthy, and everything was good. But I wasn't happy with me. So I went on a low-fat diet and started exercising. I wasn't feeling competitive the previous year; I was just playing golf and that's all.

—NANCY LOPEZ, IN *GOLF MAGAZINE* (1997)

What's the worst thing that can happen? I can hit it out of bounds and lose two shots. But I have a little money in the bank, my wife still loves me, and the dog won't bite me when I go in the door. So the shot can't be all that important.

—DR. RICHARD COOP WITH MIKE PURKEY, "MORE CHAMPIONSHIP THINKING," IN *GOLF MAGAZINE* (1997)

Once I was able to get into the lead on Sunday, I felt like others would look and know I was on my way. The players pretty much knew me and my game. Once I started making birdies, I'd keep making them.

—NANCY LOPEZ, IN *GOLF MAGAZINE* (1997)

Pressure is a relative term. You have to stay in the present. Focus on the current shot. If you think of your score, you're putting undo pressure on a series of shots you haven't even hit yet. It's amazing that when I play with a surgeon, let's say, who is terrified over a three-foot putt yet is perfectly calm when he is operating on a patient in a life and death situation. Golf isn't pressure, it's fun. I get people to think in the present.

I've found that golf "pressure" does reveal a person's character. It brings out the best and the worst in people. Self-management on a golf course is important. When I teach, I try to relate the game to how the golfer manages his life in areas where he is successful. Don't allow this game to consume you. Yet some low handicappers, for instance, have trouble handling golf. They can be overly analytical. I guess it's paralysis by analysis.

—STEVE FRIEDLANDER, GENERAL MANAGER AND DIRECTOR OF GOLF, BLACKWOLF RUN AND WHISTLING STRAITS, KOHLER, WISCONSIN (2000)

Don't mistake my ability to focus for misery. I'm having a great time on the course. I've learned to smile more and show just how great fun the game is. When the competition is at its fiercest, as when Hal Sutton and I went head-to-head at this year's Players Championship, I was really intense, but I was having a ball.

—TIGER WOODS, "THE LESSONS I'VE LEARNED" IN *GOLF DIGEST* (2000)

But as far as pressure is concerned, I still think that playing in the Tour Qualifying School was the most pressure I've ever had. You only get one week for your career.

—BRUCE LIETZKE, IN *JUST A RANGE BALL IN A BOX OF TITLEISTS* BY GARY MCCORD (1997)

He has dominated the sport more than any other man has ever dominated golf. He is a man who doesn't really have a weakness which is the first time I've seen that in any real champion.

—GARY PLAYER AFTER TIGER WOODS WON THE 2000 BRITISH OPEN AT ST. ANDREWS, IN *GOLFWEEK* (2000)

Be your biggest cheerleader. Athletes in any sport need a positive attitude.

—SEAN TAYLOR, PROFESSIONAL, DUKE UNIVERSITY GOLF CLUB, DURHAM, NORTH CAROLINA (2000)

In order to deal with pressure on the golf course, your expectations must be realistic. For example, it might not be a good idea to play from the back tees unless you are a scratch golfer. Unlike tennis and other sports, you can play against a better opponent because of the handicap system. But you still have to know your limitations and strengths. Also, try to behave in the same way despite the situation. Your first shot in a tournament round should be played in the same way as the last. Don't consider one shot more important than another. Finally, preparation is the key to coping with pressure. Work on your game in the practice game and put yourself in competitive pressure situations on the golf course so you will get used to it—whether it is a PGA Tour event or a friendly bet. A lot of people avoid pressure situations. Play in as many tournaments as you can. Find out what you need to work on.

—FRED GRIFFEN, DIRECTOR OF THE GRAND CYPRESS
GOLF ACADEMY, ORLANDO, FLORIDA (2000)

Modern geneticists have yet to map the elusive chromosome that enables certain golfers to respond to intense pressure with correspondingly heightened performance. All we know is that the Nicklauses and Woodses of this world have it. And by we, I especially mean their fellow competitors.

The most telling remark of the 2000 PGA Championship at Valhalla may have been made by Steve Kaye, Bob May's caddy. May had just seized the advantage by sinking a heartstopping 15-foot down-hiller from the fringe for a birdie on the 72nd hole and the two were watching Woods stalk a slippery six-footer that would tie the score. "Partner, get ready," Kaye told the man who, if Tiger failed to make the putt, would become perhaps the biggest upset winner of the Championship in its eighty-two-year history. "We are going into a playoff. He is not going to miss."

And of course he didn't.

—SWILCAN BURNS, GOLF WRITER AND
PGA TOURNAMENT OFFICIAL (2000)

What I like most about Tiger is the way he's handled himself. He's had far more pressure to deal with than I ever did. Athletes today live in fish bowls and face constant intense scrutiny. Tiger has had to deal with pressure and the limelight since he was a small child, and I think he's handled it with unbelievable maturity.

—JACK NICKLAUS ON TIGER WOODS, IN THE EIGHTY-SECOND
PGA CHAMPIONSHIP PROGRAM (2000)

CHAPTER 13

THE RANGE: PRACTICE

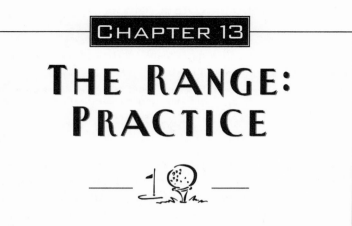

Most golfers believe that repetitive practice under simulated competitive conditions is required to sharpen one's game. In the old days professionals tended to practice by playing rather than beating balls all day. Then players such as Ben Hogan came along and relentlessly forced themselves to discipline their swing and hone their competitive skills on the practice range.

Now there are many great teaching professionals. Among them is Peggy Kirk Bell, one of the pioneers on the LPGA Tour and owner of the Pine Needles Resort in Southern Pines, North Carolina. Bell has developed a Golfari instructional program at Pine Needles. Bell relates to James Y. Bartlett in his book, *The Wisdom of the Game's Greatest Instructors:* "Our students leave with a good understanding of their golf swings, and if they don't it's their own fault! We work two-and-a-half hours in the morning and afternoon, and they go play the course. Then, from four to six in the afternoon, it's open range time, and the instructors are there to work on specific problems . . . " Regarding the golf swing, Bell claims, "It's like a ballet, a beautiful flowing motion. It's not beating at that little ball

all tight with tension. I think that golfers should practice swing more rather than just beating balls. If you develop a good, rhythmic swing, you'll become a better golfer and enjoy the game more within your limitations."

Begin with a short stiff wooden club—for two reasons; the mode of striking the ball is not quite the same with an iron club as with a wooden one, and with an iron club an unskillful player is more likely to cut fids of turf—this will by no means conduce to your popularity with other players on that green. If, even with your wooden club you should cut up turf, be careful to replace it. Golf is not agriculture.

—HORACE HUTCHINSON, *Hints on Golf* (1886)

The oldest instruction extant in the early days of the paid professional coach was to take the beginner and make him swing a club without a ball for days before he actually hit one. Then, to make him hit shots with the various clubs various distances without actually playing a game—this for a month or so. This system, a wonderful one, was based—although I never heard it so explained—upon the building in the beginner's mind of proper mental patterns, free from the obstructing strain of actual play . . .

The eight-inch golf course in your head will do wonders if you'll take the time to plant the seed of proper mental patterns.

—EDDIE LOOS, "THE EIGHT-INCH GOLF COURSE:
ESTABLISHING PROPER MENTAL PATTERNS" IN
THE AMERICAN GOLFER MAGAZINE (1924)

In golf there are three vitally important phases. You have to start off with the proper grip. Next you must take the proper stance. Then there is the swing. Put them together on the practice tee or range. Memorize each facet with your muscles. Then relax and swing it. You don't think about eating. So groove your golf swing and forget it. Why poke yourself in the eye?

—SAM SNEAD, *SAM SNEAD'S BASIC GUIDE TO GOOD GOLF* (1961)

Try this experiment. Go out and make a few practice swings without the ball—make sure your club head grazes the ground and comes through on a straight line for a few inches before and after the spot where the ball ought to be.

When this comes easy and naturally, lay down a ball. Fix the direction you want to go and step up to the ball in the same mental state that you would start to swing an axe. Think of the objective, not the physical motions necessary to attain it. Step up to hit that ball straight and true—never mind distance— just as you would drive a nail or chop a tree. You may surprise yourself.

—EDDIE LOOS, "HIT THE BALL" IN
THE AMERICAN GOLFER MAGAZINE (1922)

An excellent exercise for the golfer is to swing a weighted club. Take an old driver and weight the head with lead. Swinging that weighted club regularly every day will strengthen the hands, wrists, arms, and back muscles. Another effective but simple hand and wrist exercise comes from squeezing a small rubber ball.

—GARY PLAYER, *GARY PLAYER, WORLD GOLFER*
WITH FLOYD THATCHER (1974)

Timing is instinctive, when you get right down to it. There's an
open window. You are about forty feet from it. Can I tell you
how to throw the ball through it? . . . It's an instinct cultivated
by practice.

—STEWART MAIDEN TO O. B. KEELER, "THE MOST COMMON
FAULTS" IN *THE AMERICAN GOLFER* MAGAZINE (1922)

There is no need for balls. My first concern is to teach you the
golf swing. If you will give me patient attention, I shall put you
on the right road—only a short way to begin with, but a yard
on the right road is worth a mile on the wrong road. At least
50 percent of golfers still play golf hopelessly after years of
practice. If you are wise, you will be warned in time.

The pleasures of golf are increased a thousandfold when it
is played correctly. Those who merely knock the ball about,
trusting to luck more than guidance, miss all the charms and
pleasures of the game.

—ALEXANDER "SANDY" HERD, "THE THREE TYPES OF PUPIL: WHICH
ONE ARE YOU?" IN *THE AMERICAN GOLFER* MAGAZINE (1923)

There is no such thing as a "natural born" golfer. One may
have natural native ability, but there isn't a fine player in the
game of golf today who hasn't spent many hours on the practice
tee. The professionals realize that an hour spent in practice can
generally reward them with more valuable information about
the golf swing than four hours of playing on the course . . . It
takes a rare individual, however, just to practice for its own
sake. You should have something for which to practice.

—GARY WIREN, *GOLF* (1971)

"This isn't going to hurt a bit," I tell the ball under my breath. "Sambo is just going to give you a nice little ride." Or I might say, "Hello, dimples, I see you're sitting up fat and ready; let us have some fun . . . " By acting as if the ball is human, I distract myself—leaving no time for thoughts of this and that. Sometimes the ball looks back at me and seems to say, "Okay, Sam, but treat me gently!" That's a ball that's friendly, the kind that will go for you . . . Get charming with your golf ball if you want pars and birdies.

—SAM SNEAD, *THE EDUCATION OF A GOLFER* (1962)

The most important advice I'd give any woman just starting to play is get the fundamentals correct. It's a bad mistake simply to pick up a club and start swinging. If you can afford them, lessons from a competent pro will be worth their weight in birdies; if money is a consideration, join a group to take lessons.

—LOUISE SUGGS, "IT'S ALL IN THE HEAD" IN *GOLF FOR WOMEN* (1961)

The best way to practice short shots with the pitching wedge is to stand behind a bunker about 10 or 20 yards from the edge of the green. Then discover through trial and error just how much power it takes to get the ball to the green. Then move farther out until you reach your maximum distance for accurate shots. To determine how far a ball will roll, you should practice landing the ball on a specific spot.

—DOUG FORD, *THE WEDGE BOOK* (1963)

You can spend the winter on an inside practice range just learning how to hit different clubs. You don't have to be outdoors to learn and you don't have to be in a hurry. Take your time. Get better at hitting each club one by one.

—SALLY LITTLE, IN *A WOMAN'S GOLF GAME*
BY SHIRLI KASKIE (1982)

Go to the practice putting green and practice those putts that are really the important ones, the five- and six-footers. Those are the ones that you are expected to make and that you expect yourself to make. When you don't, your confidence fades and with it your concentration. Practice them so much that when you are on the golf course you just think of the basics.

Go to the practice range, tee the ball up, and learn to get it airborne. Develop your tempo with the ball on the tee. When you get all the balls flying off the tee, then put the ball down on the ground. When you can consistently hit all the balls solidly with the seven iron, switch to the five iron.

—MARLENE FLOYD, IN *A WOMAN'S GOLF GAME*
BY SHIRLI KASKIE (1982)

As much as possible make your practice sessions simulate the real game. Hit from the grass when possible; use a target on all your shots; alternate the clubs, sometimes going from a wood to a short iron as you would in the playing of a hole; imagine that you are playing a particular shot on a hole at your home course; then watch the result.

—GARY WIREN, *GOLF* (1971)

A whole lot of the art of putting depends upon judgment, nerves, a sense of touch, and as much as anything else, upon luck. But by far the most important part is a sound stroke, by means of which the ball can be struck smoothly and accurately most of the time. Judgment of the speed and slope count for very little without the stroke to back it up.

For this reason, there is no finer practice for developing a reliable putting stroke than putting without a hole—just dropping a number of balls on a green or carpet and stroking them back and forth. Relieved of the need for finding and holding the line, the entire attention can be given to the club and the manner of swinging it.

—BOBBY JONES, *BOBBY JONES ON GOLF* (1966)

Before each round I suggest you putt some four-footers to get the feel of your putter and of your stroke. Practice from as many different positions and over as many different rolls as possible. Don't just stand there and hit away at random. Take a look at the rolls and try to figure them out.

—BILLY CASPER, *GOLF SHOTMAKING WITH BILLY CASPER* (1966)

The easiest way to learn is through imitation. Swinging a club is such an unnatural move that imitating someone who hits the ball well can be an easy way to learn. You can watch someone and say to yourself, "I don't follow through like she does." And so you try to do what she does.

—BETH DANIEL, IN *A WOMAN'S GOLF GAME* BY SHIRLI KASKIE (1982)

Whenever I have a five-footer, with a lot of pressure on it, I just
kind of put myself back on the putting green. I stand over the
ball and concentrate on keeping the putter low and slow, back
and through, keeping my stroke smooth. I concentrate totally
on what I have to do in order to erase the pressure I might feel.
—NANCY LOPEZ, IN *A WOMAN'S GOLF GAME*
BY SHIRLI KASKIE (1982)

I prepared four months in advance for the [Qualifying] School
by hitting one thousand balls a day. To this day, I do not know
what I was working on, but somebody, probably an elder,
monastic, lost soul of the soil, encouraged me to hit one thousand balls a day if I ever was going to "make it." I counted to
one thousand armed only with my clubs, lunch, and some
Band-Aids. I learned the greatest lesson of my life there in that
hole. Discipline. The very act of getting up on my own and
trudging down to the range and hitting balls from eight in the
morning till dusk with only fifteen minutes reserved for lunch,
when I should have been out chasing girls, proved to me I was
nuts at an early age.
—GARY MCCORD, *JUST A RANGE BALL IN A BOX OF TITLEISTS* (1997)

In order to have a quality practice session you need a preshot
routine and you need to hit to specific targets with each club.
Too many golfers just hit balls at random on the practice range.
I advise golfers to practice drills that will help them to overcome difficulties in their game. For instance, many golfers
worry about keeping their head down and, in doing so, aren't
able to properly shift their weight to the left side. Sometimes

I have my students swing the club like a baseball bat so they will get a proper feel for weight shift. And I recommend other practice drills for this problem.

—MARIAN BURKE BLAIN, HEAD PROFESSIONAL, SEVEN OAKS, COLGATE UNIVERSITY, HAMILTON, NEW YORK (2000)

When you warm up before play, or go to the practice green for a true practice session, practice lag putting first, concentrating on stopping all putts from more than 35 feet close enough to make the putt a virtual tap-in. Practice putts of intermediate length, 6 to 30 feet, second and concentrate on rolling them at a speed that stops any that miss about 17 inches past the hole. Finish your practice with putts of less than 6 feet, focusing only on rolling them into the cup at a firm, brisk pace.

—DAVE PELZ, *DAVE PELZ'S PUTTING BIBLE* (2000)

Place two clubs like a railroad track three to four feet from the hole on a straight putt. Practice putting between the tracks to develop alignment and swing path. Repeat this drill for ten to fifteen minutes, then remove the clubs and continue to work on a variety of lengths, using one ball and your preswing routine each time.

If you have problems moving on putts or tend to be jerky in your motion, set a club against your own target leg while putting. If the club drops, your lower body has moved too much. Lighten up your hand pressure and continue practicing putts of various distances until the club remains steady during the stroke.

—JANE CRAFTER AND DR. BETSY CLARK, *LPGA'S GUIDE TO EVERY SHOT* (2000)

Remember practice can be fun. You can modify the schedule to fit your goals and your playing level. Now . . . if you're a weekend warrior who wants to improve his or her game, follow this quick road map to success:

1. Practice your swing whenever possible.
2. Make imaginary shots in front of a mirror or window.
3. Grip a club when you watch television.
4. Build a practice area in your house or office.
5. Where and when possible, hit a bucket of balls during lunch.
—GARY MCCORD, GOLF FOR DUMMIES (1999)

Overpracticing can make you a worse, instead of a better putter. Your main concern on the course is "feel." That's what you want to develop on the practice green. When you've got a good feel going, quit practicing. Don't risk losing it by getting tired or losing your concentration.

My objective when I practice putting is to achieve a fluid, rhythmic feeling between my hands and the ball in a well-timed stroke. When I get the desired sensation on six or seven putts in a row, I stop.
—JACK NICKLAUS, JACK NICKLAUS' LESSON TEE WITH KEN BOWDEN (1972)

Drill: Take your setup position without a club and let your arms hand loosely, like two soggy noodles. Swing your left arm back and through, back and through; the arm follows the body pivot in a relaxed manner . . . Allow your left arm to roll over as it would in the swing so the palm of your left hand faces the sky, like you're catching raindrops. Since your left arm initiates the rotation, it is important to do this drill with your left arm only.

Only your right arm does rotate as well but it follows. If the right side takes over, your right shoulder swings out and you vary the plane and may hit the ball left.

—ROBIN BORETTI, PGA/LPGA PROFESSIONAL,
IN *GOLF FOR WOMEN* (2000)

If you have unlimited practice time, I suggest you allocate one third of your time to putting, one third to bunker and short game play, and one third to full shots. If you have approximately thirty minutes before you start your round, spend half your time on putting and the short game and half on full shots. The fastest way to save strokes is to improve your short game.

—GREG NELSON, HEAD PROFESSIONAL, RUTLAND
COUNTRY CLUB, RUTLAND, VERMONT (2000)

When you practice, pick a target. Don't just hit balls, golf is a target game. Practice like you play. Start your practice shots by hitting wedges then work your way up to the driver. Hit five or six balls with each club. Then move to the putting green. Focus on hitting short putts in order to build confidence and a consistent stroke.

—MIKE STEIGERWALT, ASSISTANT PROFESSIONAL, PINEHURST
COUNTRY CLUB, PINEHURST, NORTH CAROLINA (2000)

For starters, you have to determine how much time you have to practice. You should practice before playing. And if you don't practice in between play, you will never improve. I don't give six days of lessons in a row to a golfer. I watch him or her practice and play rounds in between lessons. Golf is not an easy game. It is probably the most awkward sport I've played. I advise beginning golfers, especially adults, not to have unrealistic expectations when they take up the game. Have a great time. Enjoy nature. You can have a lot of fun shooting 100.

—PAUL PARKER, HEAD GOLF PROFESSIONAL, BUFFALO
DUNES GOLF COURSE, GARDEN CITY, KANSAS (2000)

I suggest the following preround practice routine:

1. Go through stretching exercises to loosen up.
2. Start hitting balls with the short clubs. Work your way up from the sand wedge to the driver. Work your way back down to the shorter clubs, hitting fewer balls per club, refining the rhythm in your swing.
3. Spend extra time on the weak parts of your game.
4. Spend 50 percent of your time on the putting green, playing bunker shots and chips onto the green.
5. When putting, start with shorter putts using one ball and work back to longer putts. In this way you will build a routine and a sense of green speed and rhythm in your swing.

—DOUG HODGE, PROFESSIONAL, GRAYHAWK GOLF CLUB,
SCOTTSDALE, ARIZONA (2000)

Weekend golfers often start a round badly and may not recover because they don't warm up well or don't know how to get their swings from the practice tee to the first tee . . .

Stretch your shoulders, stretch your neck, stretch your hamstrings, stretch your back. Stretch everything that comes into play in your golf swing . . .

Once I'm on the practice tee, I take my time going from one ball to the next. I keep one simple thing in mind: It might be swing in balance, or keep my head quiet. It's a form of self-discipline and I'm getting in quality practice time as I warm up . . .

I hit each ball to a target, to simulate real situations . . .

—TOM WATSON, *TOM WATSON'S STRATEGIC GOLF* WITH NICK SEITZ (1993)

CHAPTER 14

TIPS AND RANDOM THOUGHTS

There are many theories concerning what it takes to become a good golfer. What was it about the Morris family that enabled Old Tom to win the British Open in 1861, 1862, 1864, and 1867, and his son, Young Tom, to win the same event four consecutive times from 1868 through 1872? (The British Open was not played in 1871 because Young Tom, by winning three consecutive Opens, retired the championship belt which now resides in the clubhouse of the Royal and Ancient at St. Andrews.) In addition to Young Tom, who won his first professional tournament at age fourteen, we have had other golfing prodigies, most notably Bobby Jones, Jack Nicklaus, and Tiger Woods.

Woods, for example, had won three U.S. Juniors, three U.S. Amateurs, and all four professional majors by the age of twenty-four. And he has set the all-time earnings record in the process. After being paired with Woods in the first two rounds of the 2000 PGA Championship at Valhalla in Louisville, Kentucky, Nicklaus observed: "He's doing it with such regularity and with so much left in him. He doesn't have to extend himself at all to do what he's doing."

Driving is an art. Iron play is a science. Putting is an inspiration . . .

If you happen to be a really long driver, the fact will generally be admitted without your emphasizing it, to the annoyance of your neighbors, by always firing off your tee shot the moment the parties in front of you have struck theirs.

—HORACE HUTCHINSON, *HINTS ON THE GAME OF GOLF* (1886)

The game of golf was at least three centuries old before written rules appeared, and between 1744, when the first articles and laws of playing golf were framed, and 1873, the number of written rules increased by only seven. In the past hundred years, however, there have been far-reaching changes in methods of play, in the implements used, in greenskeeping and, above all, in golfers' attitudes to the game itself. The length and apparent complexity of the present rules reflect these changes . . .

—*THE ENCYCLOPEDIA OF GOLF*, EDITED BY
DONALD STEEL AND PETER RYDE (1975)

The spice of golf, as of life, lies in variety.

—ROBERT HUNTER, *THE LINKS* (1882)

Vardon, Hagen, and all the other early and current experts of golf in this century had the left arm perfectly straight as the ball was struck.

—HERB GRAFFIS, *ESQUIRE'S WORLD OF GOLF* (1965)

However, to sum up: Until a man has learned to keep his eye
on his ball, he will not play golf. He may be an excellent fellow;
he may be the most jovial of companions, the sagest of coun-
selors, and the truest of friends; but unless he can keep his eye
on his ball, never will he be a golfer.

—ARNOLD HAULTAIN, *THE MYSTERY OF GOLF* (1908)

Do I maintain, then, the reader may ask, that everyone ought to
have the same style? By no means; on the contrary, for you or
me to model ourselves on a champion is about as profitless as
to copy out Hamlet in the hope of becoming Shakespeare . . .
In a broad and general way, each player ought to have and has
a style, which is the reflection of himself, his build, his mind,
the age at which he began, and his previous habits.

—SIR WALTER SIMPSON, *THE ART OF GOLF* (1897)

"Par" is the score that an expert golfer would be expected to
make for a given hole. Par means errorless play without flukes
and, under ordinary weather conditions, allows two strokes on
each putting green. Par is based on yardage recommended by
the various governing bodies of the world. It should be empha-
sized that par applies to each individual hole and is governed by
the length of this hole, and not, necessarily, by its difficulty.
Difficulty is taken care of under the heading of Standard Scratch
Score in Britain and elsewhere, and Course Rating in America.

—*THE ENCYCLOPEDIA OF GOLF,* EDITED BY
DONALD STEEL AND PETER RYDE (1975)

You will find it pleasanter, and in the end more polite, to be rude enough to say "No," should a man whom you particularly dislike offers to play a round with you. In the course of the two hours of irritation which your weak-minded acquiescence will ensure, it is probable that you will be driven to say something far ruder than the curt monosyllable which your delicacy at first would not let you utter.

—HORACE HUTCHINSON, *HINTS ON THE GAME OF GOLF* (1886)

We at one time proposed to ourselves to write a golfer's progress for the instruction and warning of youth, but the work proceeded no further than the headings of the chapters which run as follows: 1. The Topped Tee Shot; 2. The Bad Lie; 3. Driven Into; 4. Passed on the Green; 5. The Black Spoon; 6. Bunkered and Picked Up.

—LORD WELLWOOD, "GENERAL REMARKS ON THE GAME"
IN *THE BADMINTON LIBRARY: GOLF* (1890)

The object of puting cut on the ball is to make it fall nearly dead—to make the stroke as nearly as possible all carry and no run. This is most useful when a bunker or rough ground lies between the ball and the hole, so near to the latter that a ball lofted over the hazardous ground by a stroke played in the ordinary way would be certain to run past the hole.

The principle of the cutting stroke . . . lies in bringing the head of the iron across that [straight] line. It may be applied to a full shot, half shot, quarter shot, or shortest wrist shot, but it will be quite sufficient to consider it as used in a short swing stroke—say the quarter stroke . . .

In playing the stroke you should stand facing much more towards the line in which the ball is to go than in the full driving stroke, the ball should be more to your right hand, and your right foot in advance of the left. Again, in direct opposition to the grip for the drive, the right hand must grasp the club more tightly than the left, for it is with the right hand, practically, that the stroke must in this case be guided . . . The more loosely the club is held in the hand the deader the ball will fall. The cut or slice is put on the ball by stretching the arms to their full length (or as near as the length of the stroke admits) as the club is raised, and bringing towards and across the body as it descends again.

—HORACE HUTCHINSON, *HINTS ON THE GAME OF GOLF* (1886)

To be a good partner in a foursome, you must combine with purely golf-playing qualities a certain discriminating insight into human nature. In a foursome you have not only to keep your own head and temper, but also to make it as easy as possible for your partner to keep his. Some partners require to be told they are playing very well, when they are really playing very badly . . .

—HORACE HUTCHINSON, *HINTS ON THE GAME OF GOLF* (1886)

If I am hitting the ball with a blank mind and a driver, I am conscious of thinking how far I want it to go. If I am swinging a mashie, I think how far I want the ball to go and what I want it to do when it gets there—roll a bit or stop short. But as to the stroke, I don't think about it, section by section, and I don't

believe anybody else does, or can . . . Swing right, and keep
your blank mind as much as you can on the shot.

—STEWART MAIDEN TO O. B. KEELER, "THE MOST COMMON
FAULTS" IN *THE AMERICAN GOLFER* MAGAZINE (1922)

As he takes his stance and addresses the ball, you may note
another Hagen characteristic. Since you took up golf you have
been told to keep your eye on the ball, but have you ever
paused to wonder which eye?

There is a master eye in golf, the same as in rifle shooting,
and in most golfers, as in most riflemen, it is the right eye.
With Walter Hagen it is the left eye, as with Bobby Jones.
Offhand, they are the two leading exponents, so far as my
observation goes, of the left-eye style of address—and it is the
style that favors the right-hand golfing swing, because with the
left eye lined on the ball the head is naturally turned slightly in
the direction the body must turn in the pivot that brings the
club back; hence there is less strain in keeping the head in one
place as the backswing progresses.

—O. B. KEELER, "THE STYLE OF WALTER HAGEN: A CLOSE
INSPECTION OF AMERICA'S LEADING PROFESSIONAL"
IN *THE AMERICAN GOLFER* MAGAZINE (1923)

Hole: The units into which a course is divided, i.e., the part of
the course from the tee to the putting surface. Most courses are
made up of 9 or 18 holes. More specifically, *hole* means the
opening four and a half inches (107.9 mm) in diameter and at
least four inches (101.6 mm) deep cut in every green into
which the ball is played.

—*THE ENCYCLOPEDIA OF GOLF*, EDITED BY
DONALD STEEL AND PETER RYDE (1975)

There are many other disadvantages that we left-handers must suffer, including the fact that they're building suburban homes closer and closer to the golf courses. The left-hander, when he dubs a shot, always lands in somebody's backyard and this isn't very pleasant when they're cooking codfish.

I think I have made my case clear. What golf really needs is a course where left-handers can be segregated like smallpox patients. It would be simple to lay out one of these courses. A golf architect can take a plan of any well-known course and build it backwards.

—RUBE GOLDBERG, "LEFT-HANDED GOLF COURSES: OUR GREATEST NEED" IN *THE AMERICAN GOLFER* MAGAZINE (1924)

Golf is the one game I know which becomes more and more difficult the longer one plays it . . .

So many golfers may for a while have the feel so that he may think he can go on playing in that way easily and naturally, but the trouble is that the moment some mental impulse or physical necessity suggests to one of his muscles that it do something else at a particular time, it is likely to yield, because the thing it is doing is not the thing he can do most easily. A player who depends upon finding the feel more or less accidentally can never hope to play consistently well, day in and out, for this very reason.

—BOBBY JONES, *BOBBY JONES ON GOLF* (1966)

He stood up and raised his automatic. There was no hurried movement. I watched as he covered the leader of the six mallards. To me it seemed a long time before he finally pulled, but he knocked the leader three feet in the air and the duck dropped, a thoroughly dead bird.

Hagen had six shells and he dropped all six ducks and there was never a hurried movement in the entire performance. It was an artistic job from start to finish. He never pulled once until he was satisfied he had the duck lined up and then with his unfaltering eye and finished touch he fired and the unhappy bird fell from the sky. Surely there is a close relationship to Hagen in a duck blind and Hagen on the putting greens.

—ROBERT E. HARLOW, "HAGEN THE ARTIST: INTIMATE OBSERVATIONS BY HIS MANAGER" IN *THE AMERICAN GOLFER* MAGAZINE (1929)

It is not solely the capacity to make great shots that makes champions, but the essential quality of making very few bad shots . . . Play the shot you've got the greatest chance of playing well, and play the shot that makes the next shot easy . . . Every golfer scores better when he learns his capabilities.

—TOMMY ARMOUR, *HOW TO PLAY YOUR BEST GOLF ALL THE TIME* (1953)

Though I really hate to inject negative thinking into golf, sometimes it pays to be realistic. The truth is that even a great golfer can't honestly expect to hit more than a few very good shots during a round of play. The golfer should develop the type of thinking that allows a pool player to plan future shots in advance. Every time you step up to a full shot, you should determine where you want your ball to finish if you should miss the shot . . .

—ARNOLD PALMER, *THE ARNOLD PALMER METHOD* (1959)

In golf, customs of etiquette and decorum are just as important as rules governing play. It is appropriate for spectators to applaud successful strokes in proportion to difficulty, but excessive demonstrations by a player or his partisans are not proper because of the possible effect upon other competitors.

Most distressing to those who love the game of golf is the applauding or cheering of misplays or misfortunes of a player. Such occurrences have been rare at the Masters, but we eliminate them entirely if our patrons are to continue their reputation as the most knowledgeable and considerate in the world.

—BOBBY JONES, IN *THE MAJORS* BY JOHN FEINSTEIN (1999)

The mental attitude in which we approach a short putt has a lot to do with our success. When we walk up to a putt of ten or twelve feet, we are usually intent upon holing it; we know we shan't feel badly if we miss, so our attention is devoted to the problem of getting the ball into the hole. But it is quite different when the putt is only a yard long. Then we know that we ought to hole it easily, and yet we cannot fail to recognize the possibility of a miss. Instead of being determined to put the ball into the hole, we become consumed with the fear of failing to do so . . .

—BOBBY JONES, *BOBBY JONES ON GOLF* (1966)

I am stumped when it comes to saying which is the hardest shot in golf for me; but I know the easiest one—the first shot at the 19th hole.

—W.C. FIELDS, IN *THE AMERICAN GOLFER* MAGAZINE (1925)

The game of golf becomes easier if, from the very beginning, we establish a definite pattern at executing each shot. Begin with lining up the ball. In all the years I've seen Louise Suggs play, I've never seen her vary her procedure of lining up the ball one iota. From the time she selects her club until she strikes the ball takes no more than fifteen seconds.

—MICKEY WRIGHT, *PLAY GOLF THE WRIGHT WAY* (1962)

Etiquette is very important on the golf course. So much so that it forms the first section of the Official Rules of Golf published by the Royal and Ancient Golf Club of St. Andrews and the United States Golf Association . . . Here are some key points . . .

- Don't walk or move while others are playing.
- Always try to be aware of others playing behind you and let them through if you are holding them up . . .
- Always be punctual at the first tee. Don't damage the tee with practice swings.
- Replace divots and repair ball marks on the green . . .
- On the green, don't walk on the line of another player's shot . . .
- State the score in a match at the end of every hole if you are the player who is down. If you are the one who is up, state the score if your opponent fails to do so.
- When marking your ball on the green, use a small coin or ball marker and place it behind the ball before picking it up . . .

—VIVIEN SAUNDERS, *THE GOLF HANDBOOK FOR WOMEN* (2000)

Self-motivation is important in golf. You can watch television and pick up little tips. Swing your putter and practice getting it on a straight line while you watch the Tour professionals. Build your hand strength while squeezing an exercise device. Or just sit in your office and mentally play a course in your imagination.

—MIKE STEIGERWALT, ASSISTANT PROFESSIONAL, PINEHURST COUNTRY CLUB, PINEHURST, NORTH CAROLINA (2000)

In order to sharpen up your short game, go out to the course at the end of the day and play it like a par-3 layout. Play your first shot on the par 4s and par 5s from within 150 yards. Think of the sequence of shots that you want to take and avoid trouble. By taking this approach you will realize how important the short game is.

—RICK POHLE, HEAD PROFESSIONAL, TACONIC GOLF CLUB, WILLIAMSTOWN, MASSACHUSETTS (2000)

You have to be aware of the nature of the golf course that you are playing. Think strategically. Our Talon and Raptor courses are target desert golf courses. You have to keep the ball in play and you have to pay attention to yardage and club selection. We recommend that the golfer play from a tee distance suited to his or her handicap. For example, the better lady golfers and 20-plus-handicap male golfers should play from our "Heather" tees, which are around 6,100 yards on the Raptor and 5,900 yards on the Talon course. The more advanced players (5 to 15 handicap) will play from the "Paloverde" tees (6,600 yards on the Raptor and 6,400 on the Talon) and scratch golfers can play from the back tees (7,200 yards on the Raptor and 7,000 on the Talon). Playing from the proper tee distance improves pace of play and makes the game more enjoyable for all concerned.

—DOUG HODGE, PROFESSIONAL, BLACKHAWK GOLF CLUB, SCOTTSDALE, ARIZONA (2000)

A controlled shot to a closely guarded green is the surest test of any man's golf.

—A. W. TILLINGHAST, *THE WORLD ATLAS OF GOLF* (1971)

I think it is so important that you associate with the right kind of people. I often hear fellows say that they don't enjoy their golf game because they're playing with this guy or that guy. For amateurs especially, golf is supposed to be fun. Why would you play with someone you know is going to make you miserable?

—SAM SNEAD, *THE GAME I LOVE* (1997)

Any time you can shoot a 62, no matter how easy the course may be, that's golf. But to my mind any time an 85–90 golfer shoots a 75, that's even better golf. That is the equivalent of a professional shooting 59. It is a fair comparison because it is impossible for the 85–90 golfers to reach the green at half the holes in two strokes on most courses . . . My hat is off to the plus-85 shooters . . .

Someone once estimated that 90 is the dividing line between a golfer and a dub. If that is true, then only 15 to 20 percent of those who play the game can accurately describe themselves as golfers.

—BEN HOGAN, *BEN HOGAN'S POWER GOLF* (1948)

It was a magnificent afternoon and the youngster, reveling in the warmth and sunshine, had been connecting pretty well with her long game. Her head tempted her having a joy shot.

Light-heartedly she went out for a big second shot to get to the green which was on the far side of a sparkling stream.

When things are going this well, there is a tendency to be overconfident and careless; the joy shot resolved into a full-blooded top that bumbled along the carpet and tottered down the bank into the water. That stroke changed the trend of the game. Having let up her concentration, the young player could not recapture it again. Suddenly the course became awfully narrow and full of trees—and the ex-champion started holing putts.
—ENID WILSON, *A GALLERY OF WOMEN GOLFERS* (1961)

An odd statistic surfaced a few years back when it was found that something like six of the PGA's hundreds of tour players subscribed to the annual Decisions-update service. At the time, it cost $25. Compare this with the amount of money they would receive for finishing even sixtieth in a tournament. A penalty stroke or two could cost thousands of dollars.
—GEORGE EBERL WONDERING WHY PGA TOUR PLAYERS AREN'T BETTER INFORMED ON THE RULES OF GOLF, *A GOOD WALK SPOILED* (1992)

But when it comes to this fascinating and frustrating game, there are a few convictions I held that are based on observations and are not to be classified as prejudices . . . One of these convictions has to do with women and golf. There's been far too much of this nonsense, so far as I am concerned, about women being inferior on the golf course. The people who make this claim are usually basing their argument on the female's physical structure. To them I say: "If a woman can walk, she can play golf."
—LOUISE SUGGS, LPGA PIONEER AND HALL OF FAMER, TO TOM SCOTT, "IT'S ALL IN THE HEAD" IN *SECRETS OF THE GOLFING GREATS* (1965)

If you were to compare a woman and a man with equal handicaps hitting a five-iron to the green, you'd probably see the man hitting his shot from 170 yards out and the woman hitting hers from about 110 to 120 yards out, more or less. This difference, however, is not important . . . The point of the game is to get the ball into the hole in the fewest number of strokes possible. Your sex does make a difference in what club you choose to make a shot, but not in the number of strokes you take to get your ball into the hole. And that's what you put on your scorecard.

—SHIRLI KASKIE, *A WOMAN'S GOLF GAME* (1982)

Here are some tips for playing in the rain:

• Keep a dry ball for driving. A wet ball dives rather than flies.
• If it is extremely wet, take your practice swings before teeing up the ball to keep it as dry as possible.
• Keep the grips of your clubs dry . . .
• While waiting for your partners to tee off, keep your club dry and return it to the bag as soon as possible after use.
• The rain can make recovery shots from the rough difficult. Don't be greedy, but get back on the fairway at all costs.
• Wet greens initially become slippery and the ball skids. As they get wetter, they quickly get less slippery and become slower.

—VIVIEN SAUNDERS, *THE GOLF HANDBOOK FOR WOMEN* (2000)

Golf economized the physical differences in individuals by requiring not only strength for good distance, but also accuracy and adeptness in the shorter strokes around the green. In short, the physical requirements for enjoyable participation in golf are not overwhelming.

—GARY WIREN, *GOLF* (1971)

But at the end of the day you're out there alone, naked in front of the world. Such is the nature of golf. There must be something in your gut in those situations, when you're coming down the stretch of a tournament. You must honestly enjoy your palms sweating, feeling as if you're going to jump out of your skin, your stomach tied in knots, your mind racking at 100 miles per hour.

—CURTIS STRANGE, "ELUSIVE TANGIBLES,"
IN *GOLF MAGAZINE* (1997)

How to play par 3s—Unfortunately, too many bogeys, double bogeys, and worse are made on the easiest holes because golfers don't plan them carefully enough . . . Distinguish between the safe part of the green and the fat part. Play for the safe part, not the fat part . . . Always tee the ball up on a par 3 . . . A good rule of thumb is to take one more club than you think you need . . .

—TOM WATSON, *TOM WATSON'S STRATEGIC GOLF*
WITH NICK SEITZ (1993)

Based on studies, putting is an entire game in itself. One of six different and distinct games that make up golf. In golf, the ball always reacts to the decisions and motions we make in the putting game, the short game, the power game, the management game, the mental game, and the physical fitness game, and your skills in these six games determine your ability as a golfer.

—DAVE PELZ, *DAVE PELZ'S PUTTING BIBLE* (2000)

I've learned that success thrusts you onto the world stage, and you have to always be mindful of your appearance—and just as important, your image. I enjoy dressing nicely and doing my own laundry, including ironing my clothes. I still haven't quite mastered the perfect crease, though.

—TIGER WOODS, "THE LESSONS I'VE LEARNED"
IN *GOLF DIGEST* (2000)

CHAPTER 15

DREAM PLACES TO PLAY

One of the fascinating things about golf is the choice of many venues to play. These might include a traditional links-land course such as St. Andrews with its huge double greens and other unique features including the famous Road Hole, the par-4 17th, considered one of the most difficult in the world. Or you might play a PGA Tour course such as the TPC Sawgrass with its infamous par-3 17th island green.

Many have waxed rhapsodic about the links, especially the course one regularly plays, as John Somerville did in the "Ballade of the Links of Rye" in 1898:

> How gay the heart is and how light
> When Beauty, Sport, and Friendship greet!
> Where all the joys of life invite,
> And warm it with their genial heat!
> Sweet is the lark's song—but more sweet
> The golf ball's whistle as it flies
> Swift toward the mark which it should meet—
> The golfer lives in Paradise.

I have just finished a round at St. Andrews with a feeling of profound thankfulness for not having committed infanticide. From the last tee my ball leaped lightly over the left ear of a small and quite unconscious boy who was walking along the road that crosses the links and leads to the shore. All day long there is a procession along it of motor cars, perambulators, children, and old ladies, and the golfer, learning perforce to be callous, drives over, round, or through them from the first and from the last tees. Mr. Horton, the starter, in his box, periodically shouts "Fore" at the people in a voice of thunder or, rather, he makes some horrific sound with no distinguishable consonants in it, but nobody pays attention and, which is more surprising, nobody is killed.

—BERNARD DARWIN, "ST. ANDREWS: OBSERVATIONS ON PLAY AT THE
    SHRINE OF GOLF" IN *THE AMERICAN GOLFER* MAGAZINE (1923)

St. Andrews, Prestwick, and Carnoustie are relics of the old natural links on which the game first became popular. To this day, nobody knows who laid them out, but even they are refinements of the earliest golfing arenas used when the game was played across country. There were no fairways, no tees, and no greens, simply agreed starting and finishing points.

—DONALD STEEL, "LINKS COURSES: NATURE'S GIFT TO GOLF" IN *THE
    WORLD ATLAS OF GOLF*, EDITED BY PAT WARD-THOMAS, CHARLES
    PRICE, DONALD STEEL, AND HERBERT WARREN WIND (1991)

On any course it will be a vital necessity to have a considerable range of teeing ground, so that each hole can be readily lengthened or shortened according to the state of the ground, and the strength and direction of the wind. This is a simple precaution which is often disregarded, and even at clubs where ample teeing grounds exist, it is quite common to find that no intelligent use is made of them. Wind and rain are disturbing factors, and unless the length of the holes is wisely regulated, it is certain that in many cases they will be temporarily robbed of their essential characteristics by the weather.

—H. S. COLT AND C. H. ALISON, *THE MODERN COURSE FRAME WORK—SOME ESSAYS ON GOLF-COURSE ARCHITECTURE* (1920)

The first purpose of any golf course should be to give pleasure, and that to the greatest number of players . . . because it will offer problems a man may attempt according to his ability. It will never become hopeless for the duffer nor fail to concern and interest the expert; and it will be found, like Old St. Andrews, to become more delightful the more it is studied and played.

—BOBBY JONES (1951)

The strategy of a golf course is the soul of the game.
—GEORGE THOMAS JR., *GOLF ARCHITECTURE IN AMERICA* (1927)

When two golfers return home after a few days' play on a new links, it is surprising how often their opinions vary as to its merits. On inquiry you will generally find that the one who is most enthusiastic in its praise has won the great majority of matches . . .

—HORACE HUTCHINSON, *HINTS ON THE GAME OF GOLF* (1886)

Prestwick holds a special place in the history of British golf because it is the birthplace of the Open Championship. Not only was the Championship held there for the first twelve years of its existence, but the idea of it originated with the club itself. Because of its limited length and short finish, because of the lack of space for car parking, practice, and all the trappings of a modern championship, the course has not been used for a British Open since 1925 or an Amateur since 1952. In a sense it may be described as a museum piece. It has retained perhaps better than any other course the basic features of golf as it was originally understood—small, hidden greens guarded by humps and hollows, blind shots over towering dunes, a burn, a wall, and bunker faces lined with sleepers [railroad ties] . . .

The course was opened in 1851 on common land where golf had been played for years and consisted of twelve holes, with three rounds constituting the Open Championship test. Six more holes were added in 1883.

—*THE ENCYCLOPEDIA OF GOLF*, EDITED BY
DONALD STEEL AND PETER RYDE (1975)

The ladies' courses at Formby, Sunningdale, and Wirral are probably the best-known clubs which are run entirely by women on their own and without any men on their committees. Formby ladies' course is hidden away in a tract of dune country enclosed by the Formby men's course. It has everything that has made big courses so famous—gorgeous golfing country, fine turf on the fairways and greens which are a delight. Like the big neighbor it has prickly thorn and pine to trap those who cannot keep straight . . .

—ENID WILSON, *A GALLERY OF
WOMEN GOLFERS* (1961)

The par-4 17th (Alps) at Prestwick is typical of many blind holes that once existed on the old links courses. It used to be considered a sporting hole, but its emphasis on the vagaries of fortune—their cruelist twist epitomized by the deep bunker below—to the almost total exclusion of skill, makes the Alps an anachronism.

—DONALD STEEL, "LINKS COURSES: NATURE'S GIFT TO GOLF" IN *THE WORLD ATLAS OF GOLF*, EDITED BY PAT WARD-THOMAS, CHARLES PRICE, DONALD STEEL, AND HERBERT WARREN WIND (1991)

In a land where beauty, poetry, conflict, and passionate belief in the individual are constantly intermingled, the Irish have found golf to be a ready expression of their character and flair for games. The enthusiasm of the players, variety of styles, and the quality of courses is remarkable. Ireland is not large, but it has several of the finest tests of golf to be found anywhere in Europe.

Except in the country itself, where local feelings might influence judgment, one would be hard-pressed to find agreement as to which was the greatest course—Portrush, Portmarnock, or County Down. Those three are not alone, for Balybunion and Rosses Point on the Far Atlantic shore, Killarney, serene on its lakeside amid the mountains, and Waterville have elements of majesty.

Of all the courses, few are blessed with the natural magnificence of Portmarnock . . . Portmarnock's moods can vary from a sternness that can be savage, to wondrous peace. In summer, with a fresh breeze sparkling the bay and stirring the dune grasses, Ireland's Eye and Lambay rising sharp from the sea, there are few more tempting places for a golfer to be.

—PAT WARD-THOMAS, *THE WORLD ATLAS OF GOLF*, EDITED BY PAT WARD-THOMAS, CHARLES PRICE, DONALD STEEL, AND HERBERT WARREN WIND (1991)

Muirfield is almost in Edinburgh's front yard, a dozen miles out along the south coast where the Firth of Forth empties into the North Sea. It is the gem of a cluster of some of the finest seaside golf courses in the world. It is the home of the Honorable Company of Edinburgh Golfers, the oldest club in existence, and of course, unlike the other stalwart Scottish links on the Open rotation, is the property of a private club . . .

The whole course lies open to fierce winds that blow off the water. There are no trees to protect it other than a copse of stunted growth called Archerfield Wood. It is exceptional golfing ground with many striking sand hills and views of the sea that make it seem part of the course.

—AL LANEY, *FOLLOWING THE LEADERS* (1968)

It is a special feeling, I think, that calls the golfer back to Scotland as the sailor is called by the sea. Take me to the grave of Old Tom Morris, a voice says. Drive me around the Road Hole. Show me where the Wee Icemon chipped it in at Carnoustie. Lead me down the long, narrow 11th at Troon where Arnie made the threes. Let me hear the groan of the spitfire ghosts at Turnberry. Carry me over the Sleepers at Prestwick. Bend me around the archery field at Muirfield. Drown me in all of these treasures of time once more in this, still another life.

—DAN JENKINS, *THE DOGGED VICTIMS OF INEXORABLE FATE* (1970)

Almost all the great championship courses of Britain and Ireland evolved on Links-land, significantly helped along in a later era by the hand of man. All the early designers remain anonymous; not so those who, along with H. S. Colt, creator of

Sunningdale, took the drastic step of moving golf inland and in so doing established golf architecture as an art.

—DONALD STEEL, "GOLF'S GRAND DESIGN" IN *THE WORLD ATLAS OF GOLF*, EDITED BY PAT WARD-THOMAS, CHARLES PRICE, DONALD STEEL, AND HERBERT WARREN WIND (1991)

Porthcawl was founded in 1891 and started with nine holes laid out on common land near the sea. However, cattle on the greens, carriage wheels, and camping were a constant nuisance and eighteen holes were planned afresh. Many years passed before their quality was appreciated and even now a first sight of the intimate little clubhouse would not suggest the presence of a championship course. Nevertheless, a more beautiful, princely beginning could hardly be imagined . . .

At Royal Porthcawl, as is often the case with British seaside courses, a high premium is placed on a golfer's ability to play accurately in spite of the elements. Finding the fairway from the tee is often only the beginning . . . Sight of the Bristol Channel from every hole is one of the pleasures of Porthcawl, but it is the wind from the sea that makes some of the holes so difficult to play . . .

—PAT WARD-THOMAS, *THE WORLD ATLAS OF GOLF*, EDITED BY PAT WARD-THOMAS, CHARLES PRICE, DONALD STEEL, AND HERBERT WARREN WIND (1991)

Few clubs other than Chantilly have longer enjoyed the blessing of two courses. In the early 1920s Tom Simpson was commissioned to lay out a new eighteen holes and to form the present championship course, known as Veneuil. Much of his work was damaged beyond reclamation during World War II and nine of the new holes were abandoned, but there is little doubt that

Simpson's work on the main course, which included reducing the number of bunkers, was the foundation of its greatness.

At first sight Chantilly gives an impression of dignity, peace, and space. Nothing is confined or cramped; there is always ample room around the greens and tees and between the holes. The course falls quietly away from the clubhouse, rather as it does at the Augusta National: All around is the great forest and nowhere is there the slightest glimpse of an alien modern world. At once the impulse to play is strong; the awareness of a demanding and beautiful course immediate.

—Charles Price, on Chantilly Golf Club, Oise, France, *The World Atlas of Golf*, edited by Pat Ward-Thomas, Charles Price, Donald Steel, and Herbert Warren Wind (1991)

One of his ideals was the possession by America of a golf course, built on the lines of the old classic links, and embodying all that is best in them. He fulfilled his own dream by making the National Golf Links of America, on Long Island . . . One or two of the holes on which he had set his heart he found more or less ready made, such as the Redan from North Berwick and the Alps from Prestwick. Others, such as the High Hole In and the Road Hole from St. Andrews were deliberately built, as it were, stone by stone.

—Bernard Darwin, "Charles Blair Macdonald" in *The Darwin Sketchbook* (writings from 1910 to 1958)

Most Britons, of whatever skill, have been brought up to regard a links course as the ideal playground, on which the standard hazards of the game are the wind, bumpy treeless fairways, deep bunkers, and knee-high rough. Most Americans think of a golf course as a park with well-cropped fairways marching like parade grounds, between groves of trees down to the velvety greens. Along the way there will be vistas of other woods, a decorative pond or two, some token fairway bunkers and a ring of shallow bunkers guarding greens so predictably well watered that they will receive a full pitch from any angle like a horseshoe thrown into a marsh.

—ALISTAIR COOKE, "THE FINE FINGER OF MANY LANDSCAPES" IN *THE WORLD ATLAS OF GOLF,* EDITED BY PAT WARD-THOMAS, CHARLES PRICE, DONALD STEEL, AND HERBERT WARREN WIND (1991)

In America, Charles Blair Macdonald created the National Golf Links, the first course of real quality built beyond the shores of Britain and Ireland, and in the years until the end of World War I some exceptional courses were nursed into existence by truly gifted men: George Crump (Pine Valley), the Fownes family (Oakmont), A.W. Tillinghast (San Francisco Golf Club), and Hugh Wilson (Merion) . . .

—DONALD STEEL, "THE BIRTH OF GOLF COURSE ARCHITECTURE: MAN TAKES A HAND" IN *THE WORLD ATLAS OF GOLF,* EDITED BY PAT WARD-THOMAS, CHARLES PRICE, DONALD STEEL, AND HERBERT WARREN WIND (1991)

It is a tough course as well as a beautiful one at Pebble Beach. Indeed, that is the impression I carry away with me from the 1929 National Amateur Championship. In the South, we have no courses suitable to compare with those architectural visions on the Monterey Peninsula, and with those I saw at Los Angeles. And even along the Eastern seaboard, and on the famed black turf of the Middle West, there seems to be nothing so fine and beautiful. I honestly believe that the California courses I have

seen, at Los Angeles and near San Francisco, and especially
Cypress Point and Pebble Beach on the Monterey Peninsula, are
the finest golf courses in the world today.

—O. B. KEELER, IN *THE AMERICAN GOLFER* MAGAZINE (1929)

Inverness is steeped in old-country tradition. When the citizens
of Toledo decided in 1903 to have a golf club, they wrote to
the capital of the Highlands and asked the Inverness Club if
they could use its name. The generous Scots not only gave that
permission but offered the Americans permission to use their
club's seal . . . During the 1920 Open, for the first time anywhere, the whole Inverness clubhouse was thrown open to the
professionals. For the first time at a championship, the professionals changed in the locker room, ate in the club's restau-
rants, and entered by the front door. In appreciation, Walter
Hagen took up a collection from all his colleagues, and they
bought a handsome clock to present to the club. It still stands,
keeping good time, in the main foyer with the following inscrip-
tion engraved on a brass plate:

> God measures men for what they are
> Not what in wealth they possess.
> This vibrant message chimes afar
> The voice of Inverness.

—*THE ENCYCLOPEDIA OF GOLF*, EDITED BY
DONALD STEEL AND PETER RYDE (1975)

The modern practice of staggering flanking fairway bunkers is
perfectly illustrated by Pete Dye's 1969 design for the 13th at
Harbour Town. The ideal tee shot must be threaded between

the left-hand bunker and a lone oak tree but kept out of the right-hand bunker. Dye also made interesting use of trees, a device which is becoming increasingly popular by using two oaks to guard the entrance to the green.

—DONALD STEEL, "THE MODERN ERA: THE LAND YIELDS
TO THE MACHINE" IN *THE WORLD ATLAS OF GOLF*,
EDITED BY PAT WARD-THOMAS, CHARLES PRICE,
DONALD STEEL, AND HERBERT WARREN WIND (1991)

The site chosen for Hirono was in every way ideal. Twelve miles to the northwest of the port [of Kobe, Japan] it was, in a contemporary description, "dotted with many pretty ponds, winding streams, running rivulets, pine woodlands, ravines, and gentle undulations." The materials were at hand for an architectural artist, the Englishman Charles Alison. And the course he designed in 1930 remains unaltered to this day.

At Hirono Alison took advantage of the terrain to arrange, as at Sunningdale and St. George's Hill (where he had worked with Harry Colt), several splendid carries from the tees. He planned intriguing greens at the end of generous fairways and sprinkled the course with bunkers of the type that in Japan bear his name to this day. In every way it was a piece of Berkshire transplanted in the Orient.

—PETER THOMSON, *THE WORLD ATLAS OF GOLF*,
EDITED BY PAT WARD-THOMAS, CHARLES PRICE,
DONALD STEEL, AND HERBERT WARREN WIND (1991)

I shall never forget my first visit to the property that is now Augusta National. The long lane of magnolias, through which we approached, was beautiful. The old manor house, with its cupola and walls of masonry two feet thick, was charming. The rare trees and shrubs of the old nursery was enchanting. But when I walked out on the grass terrace under the big trees behind the house and looked down on the property, the experience was unforgettable.

—BOBBY JONES, *GOLF IS MY GAME* (1966)

The 8th—the Ultimate Temptation: It is a stiff test of a golf architect's skill to ask him to make something out of a hole of only 300 yards; few holes on earth of this length can be reckoned to be anything other than stop-gaps. The par-4 8th hole on the Royal Melbourne championship course is a grand exception. Granted the designers, Alister Mackenzie and Alex Russell, had a perfect piece of land to work with but the result nonetheless is quite unique. It makes the sternest demands on good and bad players alike, and no matter what the weather conditions scores here can vary from two to ten.

In golf course design, two interesting themes run counter to each other. The one rather standard principle, that the farther one hits and the nearer one approaches the target the finer becomes the margin of error, is cleverly offset by the axiom that the more finely judged second shot gets progressively more difficult the further one falls short of the green . . . The real art of a short par-4 is found in the 8th at Melbourne. It is a bold and confident player who attempts to drive the enormous bunker in hope of leaving a short pitch to the green for the chance of a birdie.

—PETER THOMSON, *THE WORLD ATLAS OF GOLF,*
EDITED BY PAT WARD-THOMAS, CHARLES PRICE,
DONALD STEEL, AND HERBERT WARREN WIND (1991)

These greens are perfect. We just hit onto number 1 and rolled over the green. Chipped back and then three-putted. They're perfect.

—PAMELA EMORY, "OAKMONT PREPARES FOR THE
1992 WOMEN'S OPEN" IN *GOLF DIGEST* (1992)

What makes Pine Valley so difficult is that the course was carved into the Pine Barrens, so scrub pines vie with sand for dominance. One bunker is affectionately called "Hell's Half-Acre" but it really covers three times that much sandy-scrubby area. Some say the course has more sand than most beaches, but it's the proportion and arrangement of sand and "grun-gle"—a combination of scrubby, knotty, twisting scotchbroom and honeysuckle, cacti and imported heather—that gives the course the look of a testing ground for a ballistics company.

In addition to the volume of sand, it's the condition in which it's kept—or, more accurately, not kept—that is alarming to most who play there for the first time. Pine Valley is one of the few places where a caddie doesn't bother raking a bunker after his player extricates himself. Sand occupies such a large area of the course it would be a full-time job and increase playing time considerably if a caddie were expected to clean up after his player successfully returned to the terra firma of the fairway.

—PAMELA EMORY, "PINE VALLEY: PAR EXCELLENCE"
IN *PHILADELPHIA* MAGAZINE (1991)

Paraparaumu Beach is an antipodian phenomenon—a real seaside links. Thirty-five miles north of Wellington in New Zealand's North Island. It is reached by a winding, circuitous route overlooking the Tasman Sea and the sentinel off-shore island of Kapiti . . .

As at many other holes at Paraparaumu, nature has played a great part in the creation of the 13th. Just like the very oldest courses on which the game of golf was born, it has many humps and hollows—some of them massive—and is most spectacular. On a sunny day the view from the tee ground is unrivaled in golf. The rough is splashed with the green and yellow of broom and the green can be seen against a backdrop of distant snow-capped mountains. The invitation there is to enjoy it and thrill to its stout golfing challenge.

—PETER THOMSON, *THE WORLD ATLAS OF GOLF,*
EDITED BY PAT WARD-THOMAS, CHARLES PRICE,
DONALD STEEL, AND HERBERT WARREN WIND (1991)

I know no better golf course anywhere in the world, nor one where a warmer welcome waits. To the superficial eye, Hoylake, with its ugly red villas, may not be a place of beauty. I love it all—down to the white posts and rails in front of the clubhouse . . . And whatever anyone may say, Hoylake can look lovely when you are out practicing all by yourself somewhere near the sandhills when the summer dusk is coming on and the lights are beginning to twinkle in the houses.

—BERNARD DARWIN, "A PROUD CLUB AND AN
'HEROIC GOLF COURSE'" IN *THE DARWIN
SKETCHBOOK* (WRITINGS FROM 1910 TO 1958)

The professionals have an enormous regard for Portmarnock, which more than once they have named the first course on the European Tour. It is the essential features of the links that so appeals to them—blind shots are but nonexistent, the generous and flattish fairways minimize capricious bounces, and the greens are relatively placid, so that the pure mechanics of the putting stroke hold sway.

—JAMES W. FINEGAN, *EMERALD FAIRWAYS AND FOAM-FLECKED GREENS* (1996)

The Royal Liverpool Golf Club! A name to conjure with in the golfing world! A name that recalls great players, great championships and much golfing history during the past sixty-nine years. What changes these years have wrought in that sandy wind-swept strip of turf! What master golfers have battled with the problems of Hoylake golf! From the days of Young Tommy Morris, the champions of each successive generation have journeyed to the Royal Liverpool Golf Club in search of fresh laurels to be won on its famous links, blown by mighty winds, the most difficult of all golfing hazards.

—GUY B. FARRAR, "AROUND GOLF" IN *THE DARWIN SKETCHBOOK* (WRITINGS FROM 1910 TO 1958)

Tenison was the hardest "easy" course I ever played. It had only one bunker—to the left on the 18th hole on the East course—but it had such length and such character that it didn't need any. The many trees made it a very difficult course. When the U.S. Publinx Championship was played at Tenison, they let the rough grow, and the winning score was something like 13 over par. It has big greens, but it's just so difficult. It was a perfect place to sharpen my game.

—LEE TREVINO REMEMBERING TENISON PARK GOLF COURSE IN DALLAS, *THE SNAKE IN THE SAND TRAP AND OTHER MISADVENTURES ON THE GOLF TOUR* (1985)

One of the first places I would go to get away from it all—
the remoteness of the setting and the quality of golf are an
unbeatable combination . . . The opener, with its tee shot over
a corner of the beach, is the game's best, and there are several
other holes going out which would hold their own on any golf
course . . . It's probably one of the few Scottish links unchanged
by the pressures of international tourism. For that alone, everyone should see it.

—TOM DOAK ON THE MACHRIHANISH GOLF CLUB,
MACHRIHANISH, ARGYLLSHIRE, SCOTLAND,
THE CONFIDENTIAL GUIDE TO GOLF COURSES (1994)

The muni was a petri dish of smells. The summer days were
filled with smog and sweat. The dingy clubhouse was musty
and dank. The old head coach was awash in scotch. When he
passed it was enough to make a young man drunk. Plaids were
prevalent as Gorden redeemed his past.

—GARY MCCORD DESCRIBING RIVERSIDE (CALIFORNIA) MUNICIPAL
GOLF COURSE, *JUST A RANGE BALL IN A BOX OF TITLEISTS* (1997)

Nobody could claim that the little town of Carnoustie has
beauty or presence. It is a small watering-place set in a sandy
bay which is absolutely safe bathing for children; indeed it is
a perfect resort for toddlers, paddlers, and sand castlers. It is
an unpretentious, friendly spot, ideal for a family holiday. You
expect it to have a nice little golf course that will flatter father's
handicap—and you will find that it has a course of real magni-
tude and grandeur. Big words are needed to describe this
course. It is on the big scale. No professional has broken 70
there in two championships . . .

There is a tremendous sense of spaciousness, without gross width. I mean that the course covers a vast tract of sandy country and that it moves round to every point of the compass in a long loping and striding way. It is not an all out-and-homer. You do not more than nod two or three times to the players ahead of you. Yes, it is a giant of a course, and like a giant it can flick you to perdition with its little finger. But on the whole it is a friendly giant who prefers not to show his strength but to defeat you by wiles . . .

—HERBERT WARREN WIND, *CARNOUSTIE*

There's always one thing to look forward to—the Sunday morning round at the old East Lake with nothing to worry about when championships are done.

—BOBBY JONES, FROM "DOWN THE FAIRWAY" IN "JONES RETIRES FROM BATTLE" BY BERNARD DARWIN IN *THE DARWIN SKETCHBOOK* (WRITINGS FROM 1910 TO 1958)

One of the largest memberships in the world enjoys the trials of the Durban Country Club course, automatic choice whence the South African Open is held at Natal. At first site it seems undemanding, but many hazards are apparent only when the wind gusts off the ocean—across the sandhills which support the elevated tees and greens, and over the undulating fairways on the lowland part of the course . . .

To see the Country Club course at its best, it must be experienced in all its moods—especially in the wind, which blows often and puts a green out of reach of two shots when it could have been hit with a seven-iron only a matter of hours before. Suddenly all the bunkers then begin to make sense.

—PAT WARD-THOMAS, *THE WORLD ATLAS OF GOLF*,
EDITED BY PAT WARD-THOMAS, CHARLES PRICE,
DONALD STEEL, AND HERBERT WARREN WIND (1991)

A course with definite seaside flavor, its exposure to the wind and lack of fairway irrigation can make for some interesting shots after a long summer, as we saw during the 1995 Amateur. Its great history and unusual bunkers (dramatic flashes of sand divided by narrow grass fingers, retrofitted onto the faces of what were originally large oval caverns) also certainly give it charm.

—TOM DOAK ON THE NEWPORT COUNTRY CLUB IN
RHODE ISLAND, *THE CONFIDENTIAL GUIDE TO GOLF* (1994)

Nestled in the high Sonoran Desert at the base of the McDowell Mountains, the 2,400-foot elevation offers crisp, clean air and spectacular vistas. While the desert may remind the first-timer of a moonscape, the target-golf concept of turf tees, landing areas, and greens interspersed with transitional areas on their way to real desert soon becomes as familiar as a conventional course . . .

—JOHN GORDON DESCRIBING TROON GOLF
AND COUNTRY CLUB, SCOTTSDALE, ARIZONA,
THE GREAT GOLF COURSES OF AMERICA (1997)

The opportunity to carve out Teeth of the Dog was a once-in-a-lifetime experience. The land was scintillatingly beautiful, but most of it was bare coral rock and limestone . . . Without the

proper heavy machinery to crack the coral, the tireless Domin-
ican crew used sledgehammers, pickaxes, and chisels. We also
tied a large steel bar behind one of the small bulldozers so the
Dominicans could slam the bar into the coral, breaking off
larger points to smooth the surface . . .

In the late fall of 1971, the course, which featured seven
holes on the sea, was ready for play. The front nine holes were
gentle in their "links" way of sloping off onto the rocky beaches,
while the back nine appeared to have been molded out of solid
coral rock.

—PETE DYE, *BURY ME IN A POT BUNKER* WITH MARK SHAW (1995)

The 16th at Cypress Point is quite possibly the most beautiful golf hole in the world. Both tee and green are perched
above the ocean and the roar of the surf drowns all other
sounds as the sea surges in to foam white against the gray
rocks below. The green is lush and circled by sprawling
traps of dazzling white sand and beyond, all the way to the
horizon, is the blue Pacific.

Officially, the 16th has a par of three. But everybody
who has ever made a par on it has walked off the green
feeling he has made a birdie. It should be a par-4, it can
be a par-8 . . .

—CHARLES PRICE ON THE CYPRESS POINT CLUB, PEBBLE
BEACH, CALIFORNIA, *THE WORLD ATLAS OF GOLF*,
EDITED BY PAT WARD-THOMAS, CHARLES PRICE,
DONALD STEEL, AND HERBERT WARREN WIND (1991)

The only Ross course that you can be sure got 100 percent of
Donald's attention is Pinehurst No. 2—unquestionably his mas-
terpiece, and a certifiable work of genius—which he had the
luxury of evolving on the ground over a period of thirty years.

The intricately contoured greens and approaches that are the makings of the course weren't there originally, you see, because the original Pinehurst No. 2 had sand greens, no one yet having figured out how to make Bermuda into a good putting surface.

—TOM DOAK, *THE CONFIDENTIAL GUIDE TO GOLF COURSES* (1994)

The three finishing holes at Saranac are a fine way to end the round. The 200-yard par-3 16th has a tee shot over a pond and swale up to an elevated green flanked by large traps. You have to reach the green in the air, because a bank in front of the green tends to stop short shots cold. If you miss too far to the left or right, the ball will be in the bunker or the woods.

The 423-yard par-4 dogleg-right 17th entices you to cut the dogleg, but if you miss the ball will kick down a slope and possibly be out of bounds in the trees. If your tee shot is too far left, you have lost distance and face a shot, to a deep green protected by bunkers, out of difficult rough.

The finishing hole is a beautiful 532-yard par-5 with trees on the right from tee to green . . . The tee shot should be hit to the center or right-center to roll down a hill. Regrettably, the golfer is usually left with some sort of a downhill lie or is on level ground but short. The second shot is to a flat area in a valley, and the approach is uphill to a beautiful well-trapped green backed by a banked amphitheater . . .

—ROBERT MCCORD DESCRIBING THE SARANAC INN GOLF AND COUNTRY CLUB COURSE, SARANAC INN, NEW YORK, *THE BEST PUBLIC GOLF COURSES IN THE UNITED STATES, CANADA, THE CARIBBEAN AND MEXICO* (1996)

Eighteen dramas, some tragical, some farcical, in every round; and in every round protagonist and deuteragonist constantly interchanging parts. No wonder the oldest golfer does not tire of his links, any more than the ardent musician tires of his notes . . .

And when the curtain is rung down and the 18th flag replaced, instead of a cigar in a hansom, or a whisky and soda at a crowded bar, or a snack at a noisy grill-room, there is the amicable persiflage in the dressing-room or the long quiet talk on the veranda.

—ARNOLD HAULTAIN, *THE MYSTERY OF GOLF* (1908)